POTTERY OF THE AMERICAN INDIANS

HELEN E. STILES

Has Also Written

POTTERY OF THE ANCIENTS

"An externally beautiful, profusely illustrated book for children, of the junior high school age-group. Young readers will probably learn much from the illustrations alone. . . .
— *The Classical Outlook*

"It is surprising how much a child at school or at home can learn of the customs of nations from their pottery, through this delightful little book. . . . Nowhere is there a sign that this is a textbook. It is simply a little history of pottery, good for extra reading at school or good to own and enjoy, even for grown-ups, who will find the many photographs unusually well selected."
— *New York Herald Tribune*

"Should interest art teachers and fairly advanced art pupils. Profusely illustrated, and might well serve as a substitute for some museum excursions." — *American Childhood*

"This is a valuable book for devotees of general culture, especially with the growing emphasis everywhere upon anthropology and sociology. It traces the elder nations' expression of themselves and their history in the designs of their pottery."
— *English Journal*

"An elementary record of ancient ceramic art from 3000 B. C. to the 17th Century. While the text gives only a surface treatment of such an inclusive and fascinating subject, it brings together, in comparatively few pages, the essential facts that most students of ceramic history will find both entertaining and helpful."
— *American Ceramic Society*

"The author has made an exhaustive study of ceramics and condensed it to the most practical point . . . the halftone cuts are numerous and splendidly executed. Supporting Miss Stiles is the well-known Professor of Ceramic Art at New York State College of Ceramics, Charles M. Harder. It would seem that . . . with a copy of *Pottery of the Ancients*, teachers should be well-equipped to carry on an intelligent and interesting course in the Art of the Ancients." — *School Arts Magazine*

Funeral urn. Oaxaca, Mexico. Zapotec culture. Tiger God.

POTTERY OF THE AMERICAN INDIANS

BY HELEN E. STILES

Illustrated with Halftone Photographs

ENDPAPERS, JACKET AND LINE DRAWINGS
BY MARION DOWNER

New York E. P. Dutton & Co., Inc. 1939

PRINTED IN U.S.A.

First Edition

S. A. Jacobs, The Golden Eagle Press, Mount Vernon

ACKNOWLEDGMENTS

MANY intensive studies have been made by scientific people regarding all phases of Indian life, both past and present. The study of Indian pottery has not been neglected, but in the main has been written for the scientist or the advanced student of archaeology, ethnology, or art. The Annual Reports of the Bureau of Ethnology are frequently concerned with such studies on the subject of Indian pottery. These reports are to be found in libraries throughout the country.

It has been my task and pleasure to present outstanding points of interest which, together with the photographs so generously supplied by various museums, may lead to a detailed interest and further study of this most fascinating subject.

To acknowledge all the help that I have had along the way would fill many pages. Encouraged by my friend James A. Branegan, who for many years has had an intense interest in the native inhabitants of America, and who has had occasion to many times exhibit his valuable collection while lecturing to young people, I undertook to prepare this material.

In the libraries and halls of The American Museum of Natural History; The Museum of the American Indian, Heye Foundation; The Metropolitan Museum of Art; and the library of Teachers College, Columbia University, I have spent many profitable hours.

Again to list all source material which I have used would make a very extensive bibliography. Much of it would not be available in the average library or to the average reader. On the other hand I was amazed at the amount of literary and illustrative material which can be obtained at very little expense. There are many museums which publish the results of scientific expeditions and field work carried out by members of the museum staff. Students have made elaborate studies of the development and significance of the art motifs used by Indians in various stages of their respective cultures. Other students have prepared material showing how symbolism and symbolic design growing out of the religion of the early peoples has, perhaps, had a greater influence on Indian art than any other one significant element.

For the benefit of the teacher and the student who wish to seek further information on this subject, I would list the following sources of material. Museums in the United States which are especially interested in making collections of Indian arts and crafts are as follows:

American Museum of Natural History, New York City.
Museum of the American Indian, Heye Foundation, New York City.
Brooklyn Museum, Brooklyn, New York.
Peabody Museum, Cambridge, Massachusetts.
United States National Museum, Washington, D. C.
University Museum, Philadelphia, Pennsylvania.
Ohio State Museum, Columbus, Ohio.
Field Museum of Natural History, Chicago, Illinois.
Milwaukee Public Museum, Milwaukee, Wisconsin.
Denver Art Museum, Denver, Colorado.
Laboratory of Anthropology, Santa Fe, New Mexico.
Museum of New Mexico, Santa Fe, New Mexico.
Gila Pueblo (Private Museum), Globe, Arizona.
Arizona State Museum, Tucson, Arizona.
Museum of Northern Arizona, Flagstaff, Arizona.
Southwest Museum, Los Angeles, California.
San Diego Museum, San Diego, California.

ACKNOWLEDGMENTS

Many times I have had occasion to use material written by Carl E. Guthe, University of Michigan, Ann Arbor, Mich.; Herbert J. Spinden of The Brooklyn Museum, New York; George C. Vaillant of The American Museum of Natural History, New York City; and Kenneth M. Chapman of The Laboratory of Anthropology, Santa Fe, New Mexico. These men have been tireless in their efforts to place before the public a real understanding and appreciation of Indian art. Kenneth M. Chapman has specialized in research relating to the pottery of the Pueblo Indians, and has written two volumes entitled *Pueblo Indian Pottery*. In 1938 he released a third book entitled *Pottery of Santo Domingo Pueblo*.

To Kenneth M. Chapman I am indebted for his kindness and willingness to answer my many requests through correspondence, and for reading my chapter on pueblo pottery.

In 1924 and 1925 Ruth L. Bunzel observed potters at work in various pueblos of the Southwest. She prepared a book entitled *The Pueblo Potter* which was published by the Columbia University Press, New York, 1929. This book is "A Study of Creative Imagination in Primitive Art" and contains excellent illustrations of pottery designs and design elements. There are 94 Zuni design elements, all described, 19 Hopi designs, and 43 San Ildefonso designs as drawn by Julian, Abel, or Juan.

To understand the present and to prepare for the future we must know something of the past. To know is to appreciate. It is with this in mind that I wish to present this little book, hoping that it may awaken in the student a larger measure of understanding and appreciation of the Indian and his age-old craft of potting. The study of Indian pottery has particular significance in that its history goes back to early primitive times, and the making of Indian pottery has been carried on continuously ever since.

ACKNOWLEDGMENTS

I was particularly impressed with the following passage from *The Rain-Makers* by Mary Roberts Coolidge quoted here by permission of Houghton Mifflin Company, the publishers:

"The alien who would understand Indian behavior must first see himself in a measure as he appears to the native. He must exercise humility and have a patient willingness to learn. Above all he must pay the respect to Indian ideas, manners, and observances which is due to an ancient, deep-rooted social order. Primitive and strange they may be, but none the less profoundly expressive of men's earlier efforts to adjust themselves to an overwhelming Universe and to build up an orderly Community."

HELEN E. STILES

April, 1939

SOURCES OF ILLUSTRATIONS

Frontispiece — *American Museum of Natural History, New York City.*

Pages: 25, 30, 31, 34-37, 75 (bottom), 85 (top), 90 (top), 91 (top and bottom), 96 (center and bottom), 97, 111, 114, 115, 122 (top), 123 (bottom), 159 (bottom).
— *Museum of the American Indian. Heye Foundation, New York City.*

Pages: 42, 45 (bottom), 54 (top: l.), 55 (center and bottom), 59, 62, 63, 67, 70, 74, 75 (top and center), 84 (top), 85 (bottom), 90 (center and bottom), 92, 93 (right and bottom), 95, 96 (top), 104 (top), 105, 110 (right), 113, 116, 117, 120, 121, 122 (bottom), 123 (top), 126, 157, 159 (top: r. and l.), 160.
— *American Museum of Natural History, New York City.*

ACKNOWLEDGMENTS

Pages: 44, 45 (top and center), 54 (right, center and bottom), 55 (top).

— Laboratory of Anthropology, Inc.,
Santa Fe, New Mexico.

Page: 104 (bottom).

— Peabody Museum, Harvard University.

Page: 110 (left).

— Carnegie Institute, Washington, D.C.

Pages: 134, 135, 137-139, 142-144.

— The Metropolitan Museum of Art,
New York City.

Pages: 146, 147, 150 (bottom), 151 (bottom), 152, 153, 158.

— Photographs by M. A. Dresskell,
Teachers College, University of Columbia,
New York City.

Pages: 127, 150 (top), 151 (top), 154.

— Photographs by J. T. Johnson,
Kent State University, Kent, Ohio.

Pages: 84 (bottom), 89, 91 (center), 93 (top: left).

— Courtesy Dr. Julio Tello,
Museum of Archaeology,
Lima, Peru.

CONTENTS

POTTERY OF THE AMERICAN INDIANS

To JIM
whose interest
in all things
Indian
encouraged me
in this undertaking

Prayer for Rain

White floating clouds,
Clouds like the plains,
Come and water the earth.
Sun embrace the earth
That she may be fruitful.
Moon, lion of the north,
Bear of the west,
Badger of the south,
Wolf of the east,
Eagle of the heavens,
Shrew of the earth,
Elder war hero,
Warriors of the six mountains of the world,
Intercede with the cloud people for us,
That they may water the earth.
Medicine bowl, cloud bowl, and water vase,
Give us your hearts,
That the earth may be watered.

—STEVENSON, MRS. M. C.: *The Sia,**
Eleventh Annual Report,
Bureau of American Ethnology.

* Used by special permission.

 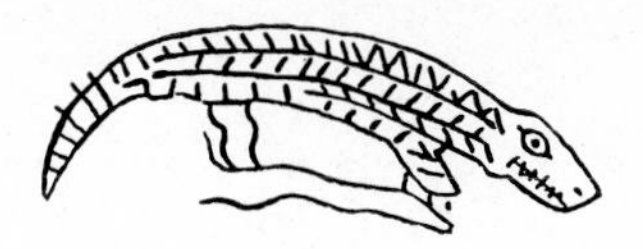 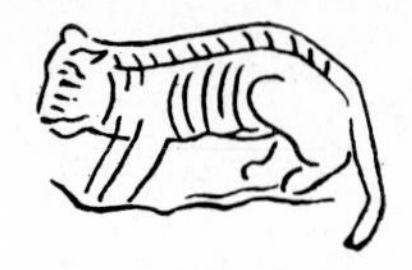

CHAPTER I

THE FIRST CLAY BOWLS

WHO made the first clay bowls? No one knows. But all over the world in many places we have found crude clay bowls and jars made by primitive man.

Far back in the past, primitive man found in nature materials for those things which he needed to make his life more comfortable. Years and years went by without many changes, but slowly man learned that many wonderful things could be made with his two hands. Mats and baskets were woven from grasses, roots, or bark of trees; bowls and jars were shaped from a lump of clay; stone tools were hammered and chipped; woods were carved; and finally metals were used.

Woven mats and clay bowls were usually the very first hand-crafts of primitive people. This was because grasses and forests grew in many places, and clay beds were found in nearly all parts of the world.

Clay is one kind of soil and the greater part of the dry land on our earth is covered with soil. In the beginning this soil was rock. Wind, frost, ice, water, snow, heat, cold, and the gases of the air have all helped to break down the rocks on the surface of the earth. After millions of years the pieces of rock became so fine that soils were formed. And because rocks are of different kinds the soils are of different kinds.

Some soils are sandy. They are just tiny pieces of clean

rock. Loam is a soil which is mixed with bits of decayed plants. Clay is a soil which, when moist, is soft and plastic. In clay the little particles of rock are so fine that they are just like dust, and nature has acted on them in such a way that the fine particles will stick together. When molded with the hands and fingers, clay will hold any desired shape. This is what we mean by plastic.

Primitive pottery — we shall speak of all things made of clay as pottery — in different parts of the world tells many things about the people who made it. All hand-crafts grew out of the daily needs of the people, all materials used were those which could be easily obtained, and all ideas of design represented the feelings of the people for beauty and rhythm, or their ideas of religious symbolism. As we discuss the different types of American Indian pottery you will understand how these things developed and what they meant to the people.

In nearly all parts of the world when savage man settled down, built homes, and planted foods he soon learned to make pottery vessels to hold his food, to store it for the winter, and to carry water from the spring or river. We know about these things because of another custom which was a natural outcome of settled life. This was the manner in which he buried his dead. Man was learning to think, to think of life and death, and then of life after death. He made elaborate preparations for death because he believed the dead person would live again.

Very often in the graves of primitive people we find pottery bowls and jars which had contained food. This food was supposed to provide for the dead person in the next world. Some tribes burned the bodies of their dead and put the

Pottery jars found at Athens, Pennsylvania. Jars as shown from Pennsylvania, New Jersey, and Long Island, N. Y. are of a very crude type although some attempt has been made at decoration and shaping.

ottery jar from Sussex County, ew Jersey. Height, 6½ inches. ecoration on neck probably ade with fingernail.

ottery jar found in Long Island, . Y. Notice impression made coarse textile.

ashes in a pottery jar. Then they buried the jar. Still other tribes had different reasons for putting things in the graves. Little pottery images have been found, and all sorts of treasures made from gold and precious stones.

Archaeologists are scientific people who spend their time in studying about the lives of ancient and prehistoric people. They have dug up old graves in many places. In certain parts of the world they have made excavations of ruined cities and have learned not only about primitive people, but about old civilizations which no longer exist. In all their excavations it is the pottery which helps them most in understanding the daily life of the people of the past.

Today, in our museums, you can see many pots, bowls, jars, and images which have been taken from the graves of early people, or from the ruins of old towns and cities.

When people first learned to make pottery it was very crude and rough. The walls were thick and little attention was paid to the shapes. It was baked in the sun and would not hold water. It was not decorated and its color was the color of the clay from which it was made.

Many early people believed that it was the gods who taught their people how to make pottery. They did not keep records and they had forgotten how their ancestors really did learn to make pottery in the first place. So when the later people did more thinking and tried to have reasons for things, their priests, who were the leaders of the people, said that the gods did everything. And the people believed the priests.

Archaeologists have learned many interesting things about the early people of Egypt, Mesopotamia, Greece, Rome, China, and other places. During the last few years they have been learning more and more about the early American Indians. They have made excavations of ruined cities, have dug up the graves, and examined the pottery, tools, and ornaments which they found in the ruins and in the graves. They have talked to the Indians of today and have tried to understand how the Indian feels and why he follows certain customs. Because of these studies we are learning more and more about the people who lived in our country before the white man came.

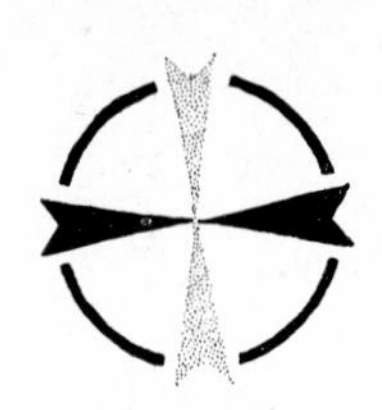

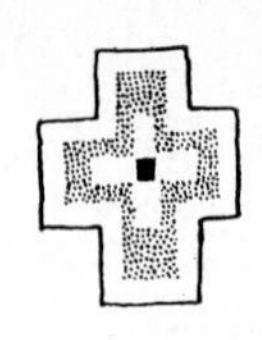

CHAPTER II

POTTERY MADE BY THE NORTH AMERICAN INDIANS

CERTAIN tribes of Indians were quite primitive at the time that Columbus discovered America. They had not learned to keep records, they wandered about from one hunting ground to another, and they did not live in real houses. Other tribes were more civilized and built houses of logs or sun-dried bricks. They lived in these houses all the year round, and near their villages they planted grains and vegetables. Some of the Indians made no pottery, some made very crude pottery, and some made very beautiful pottery.

Archaeologists have not found any pottery in the northern part of North America except among the Eskimos of Alaska. It is believed that the Indians of central and northern Canada had not gone beyond the hunter stage of civilization and used only lightweight vessels made of bark of trees, roots, or grasses. They could easily carry vessels of this type from place to place or discard them and make new ones with very little trouble. Around the St. Lawrence River and as far south as the Ohio River the pottery which has been found is very crude. In many cases it is just like rough earth and has no decoration at all. Some pieces have been found with a few lines made with a sharp stick, showing that these Indians were beginning to think about decorating their pottery.

In the region of the Great Lakes, in Pennsylvania, northern Ohio, Indiana, and Illinois the Indians made crude pottery for storage jars and cooking pots. Incised designs, stamped designs, punched designs, and applied buttons of clay were used for decoration.

In northwestern New York when the white people arrived there lived powerful tribes of Indians called the Iroquois. They decorated their pottery and were beginning to try to make interesting shapes and designs. The characteristic shape was a pot with a rounded bottom and a heavy, raised rim, or collar, around the mouth of the vessel. The rim was so shaped that humps or peaks appeared at intervals, usually four in number. Occasionally the mouth of the vessel was square. Almost always the decoration was applied to the rim only. It was simple but often quite effective. With a sharp stick or bone tool the potter made straight, parallel lines at different angles. Sometimes dots and deeper cuts are found on Iroquoisan pottery and it is believed that not only sharp sticks but blunt sticks, hollow reeds, and pieces of flint may have been used as decorating tools. Basket textiles were occasionally pressed into the moist clay to make a decorative surface, and it is possible that on some vessels a comb-like instrument was used to make incised designs. Stamped patterns were also made with a string-wound stick.

The Algonkin Indians of Manhattan and Long Island occasionally used sea shells, especially the scallop, as a decorative motif. The shell was pressed into the moist clay leaving its imprint in some form of design. It is indeed interesting

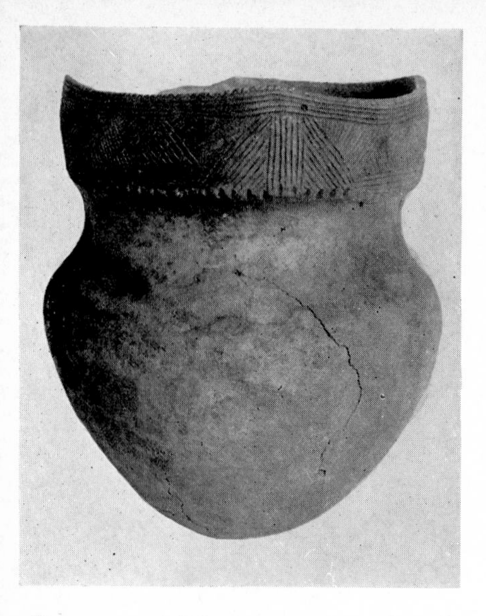

Pottery jar of Iroquoisan type found in New York City. Interesting design formed by parallel lines.

Pottery jar of Iroquoisan type, Cayuga County, New York. Notice four points on brim.

Pottery jar, restored. Clinton County, N.Y. Height, $15\frac{7}{8}$ inches. Decoration may have been made with a comb-like tool.

Pipe (stone) representing a deer's head. Notice leg and antlers. Cayuga County, New York.

Stem of calumet pipe. Oto Tribe. Bowls of various types were attached to calumet stems.

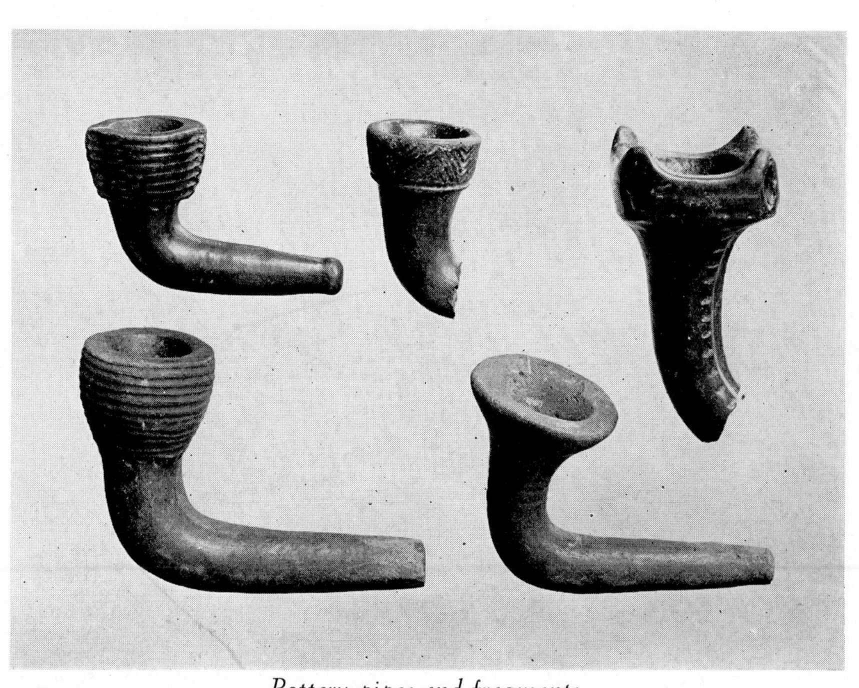

Pottery pipes and fragments.

to notice how the various objects in their environment influenced the early potters.

The Iroquois Indians made clay pipes and took greater care in making pipes than in making pots and bowls. To every Indian his pipe was a very important possession. No ceremony or treaty was complete without smoking a pipe. If he wished to show that he wanted to be friendly toward a stranger he offered his pipe to the stranger and they smoked together. Indians seldom sat around and smoked just for the pleasure of smoking. Stone pipes and clay pipes were used, and in different places we find different types.

Because the Indian felt that his pipe was so very important, he was anxious to have the best pipe he knew how to make. Many were long like a tube, others had bowls of different shapes. The Indians of southeastern Canada and northeastern United States used a ceremonial pipe with a very long stem. Early French settlers called this pipe a calumet, from the French word *chalumet* meaning a tube. Some pipes were very beautifully carved or modeled to represent figures of birds, animals, or human beings. These representations of living things are called effigies, and Indians in different parts of America have carved and modeled effigy pipes and vessels from stone, wood, or clay.

In the graves and mounds of the Indians who lived in the Mississippi Valley, archaeologists have found large pipes which were used for council gatherings of the tribe, and small pipes which they think the Indians used for special occasions in their own family gatherings.

These Indians of the Mississippi Valley, south of the Ohio River, had a more advanced culture than the Indians who lived in the northern part of North America. Their country had a milder climate, they had learned to live a more settled life, to raise corn, and to store away their harvest for the winter. Leisure time in pleasant surroundings helped them to a more advanced culture. They are called the mound builders because of the large and small mounds which they piled up in many places. Hundreds of these mounds have been located in the Ohio Valley and to the south in the valley of the Mississippi. At one time it was thought that the mound-building culture had entirely disappeared before the arrival of the white man, but further study proved that the Indians living in the southern Mississippi Valley were the survivors of the early mound builders.

People who have dug into these mounds have discovered that sometimes they are burial places but not always. Students of Indian customs believe that the mounds were used as places of worship, as signaling towers, as refuges in time of flood, or as dugouts in time of war.

Pottery of many types has been taken from different mounds, but there are two very distinctive types — effigy pottery in the form of human figures and animals, and bottle-shaped vases with incised designs.

Mounds have been found as far east as Georgia but in the main the culture of the southeastern part of the United States is considered apart from that of the Mississippi Valley.

The characteristic pottery of the Southeast was deeply incised, or cut, with a sharp stick or bone tool. This work was done before the pottery was dried or burned. All Indians who made pottery used sharp tools to make incised designs, but some of the best work of this type has been found on prehistoric pottery made by the Indians of Florida, Georgia, and Alabama. In well-spaced line designs they represented birds,

Effigy vessel. Hardman Mound. White County, Georgia.

Jar, kneeling female figure. Brown ware. Height, 7 inches. Arkansas. C. B. Moore collection.

Pottery jar. Arkansas. A simple decoration skillfully and artistically executed.

Bottle-necked jar. Incised decoration. Arkansas.

Pottery jar from Florida. Height, 6 inches. This jar looks as if it were intended to have a lid.

Bowl with deeply incised decoration. Nacoochee Mound. White County, Georgia.

Openwork pottery jar. Washington County, Florida. Height, 8¾ inches. Supposed to have been used for ceremonial purposes.

Cedar bark mat with painted decoration representing two puffins (birds). 52 x 30½ inches. Kwakuitl Tribe. British Columbia, Canada.

Storage basket. Bottom view. Diameter 4½ feet. Pomo Indians. California.

Cedar bark mat with painted decoration representing two wolves' heads. 74 x 34 inches. Kwakuitl Tribe. British Columbia, Canada.

snakes, and other animals. Scroll patterns were skillfully traced to form borders and all-over designs.

The Cherokee Indians of North Carolina are still making pottery by ancient methods, and some pieces are beautifully shaped and polished. A very interesting method of decoration is achieved with a carved wooden paddle which is pressed on the moist clay. Very often the inside of the pot is black, accomplished by their method of firing, and the outside is brown or buff, the natural color of the clay.

Out on the Great Plains lived the Buffalo hunters. They roamed over the wide open spaces following the wild herds, and did not stay very long in any one place. The buffalo supplied almost every need that these Indians had. They made very little pottery.

On the western coast of Canada and in our states of Washington and Oregon no prehistoric pottery has been found. The Indians of that area were surrounded by forests. In these forests grew many cedar trees and from these trees the natives made practically everything that they needed. Their houses were made of cedar wood, and cedar posts were carved to show the supposed relation of tribes or families to certain animals. These posts, or totem poles, stood before their houses, and beside their graves. Large dugout canoes were made from the trunks of cedar trees, many times ornamented by carved figureheads. Bowls, shovels, and boxes were made of suitable woods, and bags, baskets, hats, and mats were woven from bark or roots. Certain other trees were brought into use, but to the Indians of the Northwest the cedar was the most valuable of all the trees.

The Indians of California are famous because of the baskets they wove from fine reeds and grasses. Large baskets and small baskets with beautiful patterns in contrasting colors. These baskets were used for all sorts of purposes and many of them were painted with gum which made them watertight. The California Indians made large pottery jars for storage purposes and smaller jars for burial purposes. All their pottery was crudely made with no attempt at decoration.

There is one part of our country, however, where very fine prehistoric pottery has been found. This is the region of the ancient pueblos of the Southwest, and the pottery found in these old ruins is sufficiently important to be discussed in a section of its own.

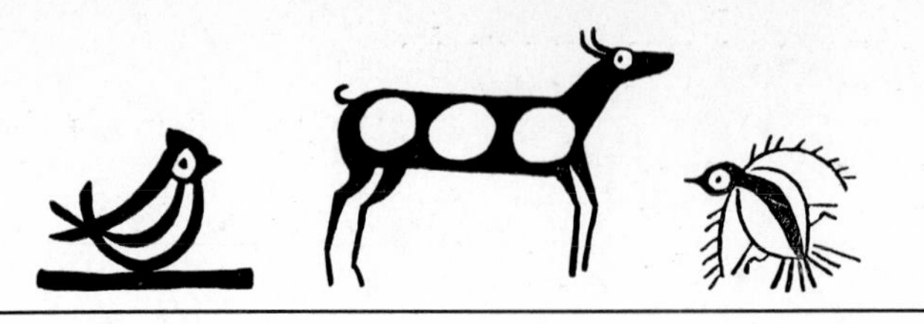

CHAPTER III

POTTERY MADE BY THE INDIANS IN OUR SOUTHWEST

IN the southwestern part of the United States are people who are making pottery today just as their ancestors made it a thousand years ago. They have never used a potter's wheel and they do all their work by hand and with a few very crude tools.

If you travel to the Southwest you will find these people living in the states of New Mexico and Arizona. Most of them live in what we call pueblos. A pueblo is really a town, or village, but usually the houses are all built together like a big apartment house. They are built of stone and adobe which is sun-dried brick. Indians of the Southwest have lived in pueblos for many years and probably made clay bricks before they made clay bowls.

At the World's Fair in Chicago during the summer of 1934 many people stopped to watch an Indian woman making pottery. This woman was Maria Martinez. During the last few years many magazines have shown pictures of her at her work. She is the very best potter in all the Southwest today. There are other women who are making really good pottery, and there are some who are making very poor pottery, but Maria's bowls and jars are the best of all. Julian, her husband, paints the designs on their pottery, and they are very busy working together. They spend all their time on this work and have no trouble in selling what they make.

In the year 1925 Dr. Carl E. Guthe made a study of pueblo pottery-making. His study was made at the village of San Ildefonso and this is where Maria Martinez lives. San Ildefonso is a Pueblo Indian town on the Rio Grande, north of Santa Fe, New Mexico.

Dr. Guthe watched Maria and other Indian potters while they worked. He went with them when they gathered their materials. He watched them prepare these materials, model their pottery, polish it, paint it, and fire it. He talked with the women and with the men, and then wrote a report showing exactly how all the work was done, and just how much time it took for each part of the pottery-making.

Dr. Guthe said that the Indians of San Ildefonso used red clay and white clay and, for their cooking vessels, a light brown clay. They did not mix their clays but used the red clay for some vessels and the white clay for others. They did, however, mix with the clay another kind of earth as a tempering material. When pure clay dries, it shrinks, and when it shrinks, it cracks. The tempering material prevents the clay from cracking. The potter must be careful to mix just the right amount of clay with the right amount of temper. If there is too much temper the clay will not stick together and the vessel will not keep its shape while it is being modeled. If there is not enough temper the vessel will crack while it is drying.

To have their pottery finished in a desired color the Indians use a slip, or covering. Each slip is made from a dif-

Pueblo Indians of the Southwest.
Painting by Arthur A. Jansson under the direction of Dr. Clark Wissler.

ferent kind of earth. At the time of Dr. Guthe's study they used two kinds of white slip, an orange-red, a red, and a dark red. Today, however, one white and the orange-red are seldom used. Water is added to the selected earth and, when it is about the consistency of rather thick cream, it is applied to the vessel with a small piece of cloth. Usually several coatings of slip are used.

Black paint is made from a plant called the guaco, or Rocky Mountain bee plant, which is a common weed and grows in large quantities near the village of San Ildefonso and in many other parts of the Southwest. The plant is gathered in the spring, placed in water, and boiled over an open fire, sometimes for a whole day. The liquid is drained off and placed in the sun to harden into a solid sticky mass, and is then stored away for at least a year before it is used. The Indians say that if it is used before that time the color on the vessel will not be a good black, but a streaky blue-black.

Maria and Julian have invented a new paint which they use for making dull designs on polished black ware. They discovered a hard yellow stone which they scrape with a knife until they have a fine powder. This powder is mixed with water and a small amount of guaco, thus making a new paint.

It has always been the custom among the Indians for the women to make the pottery and that is usually true today. Nearly all the women in most tribes make pottery, but they are not all good potters. The mother teaches her daughters, and certain ways of working are followed in each family, but the general plan is the same, at least in all the families of one tribe.

Usually, when dug, the clay is in large hard lumps. It is

Polished blackware wi matte designs by Ma Martinez. San Ildefon Pueblo. 1932.

San Ildefonso pottery. Modern.

Hopi pottery. 1875. Bird and Sun symbols.

Hopi pottery — Modern.

an Ildefonso pottery possibly 00 to 150 years old. Main lesign is a fertility symbol. Curved lines represent rainows, enclosing terraced mounains and rain blown about by vind. At top and bottom are lant motifs and at the side the nuch used feather symbol.

Hopi olla — First Mesa, Arizona.

often easier for the potter to crush these lumps and remove the pebbles before carrying it to her home. She may also sift, or winnow, the clay so as to remove even the tiniest bits of foreign material. She wants her clay to be as pure as possible and there is little use in dragging home the unnecessary weight. It may, however, be more convenient for her to haul large quantities of clay, store it at home, and use it as she needs it. Those potters who today make a business of selling their pottery have wagons or automobiles to haul the materials which they use.

In preparing the clay for use, the potter kneels on the ground before a piece of cloth on which she has piled the crushed clay. A second piece of cloth is ready to receive the sifted clay, and it depends on which way the wind is blowing just where this cloth will be placed.

The potter takes a double handful of the crushed clay and lets it sift through her fingers. The fine parts of the clay are blown over by the wind and fall on the second cloth. The little pebbles fall down in front of her. Some women toss the clay in a shallow basket, and they do this so cleverly that the fine clay falls out on a cloth and the pebbles stay in the basket.

There are other ways of winnowing the clay but the two ways mentioned above are used most often.

The fine powdered clay is now ready to be mixed with the temper, but first the temper itself must be prepared. The earth used for this purpose is very hard and sometimes it must be chopped out of the ground with an axe. Then it must be pounded and carefully cleaned until it, too, is a fine powder.

The two fine powders, the clay and the temper, are now mixed together. Once more they are sifted through the fingers until they are thoroughly mixed. Each potter knows just how much temper she wants in her pottery, but she does not weigh or measure it. She can tell by the color of her mixture, and she has experimented until she knows which mixtures have proven most successful.

After the clay and the temper are thoroughly mixed, water is added and the kneading begins. The mixture is now called paste. The paste is kneaded just like bread dough and the kneading goes on until the paste is smooth and just right for modeling.

When the potter starts to model a bowl, she takes a saucer-shaped mold. She calls it a *puki*. She sprinkles the *puki* with ashes so that the clay will not stick to it. In the *puki* she then places a round pat of paste which will form the base, or bottom, of her bowl. She presses the pat of paste down into the *puki* so that no air can get under it. She takes a lump of paste and rolls it smooth and even. She builds up the sides of her bowl with one roll after another, pressing them with her fingers to make the walls firm and strong. She shapes her bowl as she goes, turning the *puki* round and round so that all sides may be even and beautiful. She must be very careful that no air-bubble is left in the vessel, for this would cause cracking in the firing. She must watch that each roll is firmly pressed into its place so that not the tiniest crack can be there. Occasionally she may be obliged to moisten some part of her bowl, but a clever potter will use very little water while she works, for it will soften the walls and they will not hold their shape.

While the potter works on the outer surface of the bowl she supports the wall by placing her other hand on the inside. While she is working on the inside she holds her other hand against the outside, in that part of the wall where she is working.

If she is making a very large bowl she may set it aside after she has added several coils, or rolls. When the clay has partly dried and the walls have partly hardened she will work on it again. Some potters do not shape their bowls until all the coils have been added.

If she is making a very small bowl she may model the entire bowl in her hands from one lump of clay and without starting in a *puki*.

While the bowl is being shaped, the potter uses a little tool called a *kajepe*. She has several *kajepes* of different shapes and sizes, and they are made from pieces of gourd-rind. A gourd is the fruit of a certain plant and when dry it has a very hard shell. Since all the surfaces of a gourd are curved, each small piece is somewhat curved, or spoon-shaped. The potter is very skillful in her use of these little tools and with them she joins her seams, and smooths out all uneven places.

Dr. Guthe said that Maria could work faster than any other Indian potter whom he had observed, and that when he was watching her she modeled ten bowls in three hours. She worked first on one, then on another, and later came back to the first one. At the end of the third hour ten bowls of different shapes were modeled and ready to dry.

An Indian water jar is called an *olla*. Much care is taken in modeling an *olla* because the top of the vessel must be made smaller than the top of a bowl, and the sharp curve of the wall makes it more difficult for the moist clay to hold its shape. As the coils are added the sides must dry and harden somewhat before other coils are added. But the potter must watch very carefully, and occasionally moisten the edges with water so that they are not too dry when she adds the next coil. All finger marks and seams where the coils have been joined must be smoothed out by her *kajepes*.

If the vessel being modeled is to have handles the potter will use one of two methods in fastening the handles to the vessel. She may take a roll of clay, pinch the ends of the roll, and then fasten, or weld, the ends to the sides of the vessel. Whenever one piece of clay is fastened to another piece it is called welding. Sometimes the potter makes little holes in the sides of her vessel, pushes the ends of the handle through the holes, and welds them on the inside. All this must be very careful work, and it often takes quite a long time before it is finished in such a way that it satisfies the potter.

After the modeling is entirely finished, the vessels must dry in the sun. Sometimes they will dry in half a day. If the day is cloudy the vessels are dried in the house and this will take at least three days. When the potter is in a hurry she dries her vessels in the oven of a small wood-stove. Of course the potter of long ago did not have a stove and just had to wait. If she uses a stove she must keep the door open so that the moisture which evaporates from the pottery can escape. She must also watch to see that her oven, even with the door open, does not get too hot. Too much heat will change the escaping moisture to steam, which will press on the walls of the vessel causing them to lose their shape, to blister, or to crack. As the walls dry they shrink and this loosens the vessel from the *puki* in which it was built.

And now the finishing begins. The vessel has been modeled and dried, and the sides must be scraped and smoothed. For scrapers the Indians use a kitchen knife or the top of a baking-powder can. The Indians of long ago used broken pieces of pottery, sharp stones, or broken animal bones.

The scraping removes all marks left by the *kajepe* and the *puki*. It also makes the sides thinner, smoother, and more even. The Indians do not usually scrape the inside of their vessels. Some potters use a wet cloth to dampen the sides before they begin to scrape, and to give the vessel a last smoothing when they have finished the scraping.

Slipping comes next. Slip is used to make the surface of the vessel smooth, and to give it a certain color. The red and dark-red slips and one kind of white slip must be polished.

Before the slip dries, the rubbing with the polishing stone is begun. The stone is held between the thumb and the first two fingers of the right hand. Every part of the surface must be carefully polished and the potter's fingers and wrist become very tired. Small, smooth stones are used for the polishing. These stones are great treasures, for it is sometimes difficult to find just the right kind. Often a potter will have a polishing stone which had been used by her mother and her grandmother.

When the polishing with the stone has been entirely completed, a little lard is rubbed on the surface with the forefinger or with a greasy cloth. A last hard rubbing is then given with a dry cloth or a piece of skin, and the vessel is once more put in the sun to dry. Every time a piece of pottery is set aside to dry, it is covered with a cloth, for the tiniest speck of dust or fly-dirt may spoil the surface of the vessel when it is fired.

If the pottery is to be decorated with a painted design it is now ready for the painter. Quite frequently the men do the painting, but all other parts of the work are done by the women.

The paint brushes are made from the fibres of the leaves of the yucca plant which grows in the desert. Pieces of the leaves are stripped so that they are about a quarter-inch wide and five or six inches long, and one end of the strip is either pounded or chewed until the fibers are separated. They must be soaked in water to soften before they can be used.

Before the painter starts to put his design on the vessel he measures it with his fingers and plans his spacing. This is so carefully done and often so accurate that even in an elaborate design all parts of it are well balanced and beautiful. All the work is entirely freehand and can seldom be corrected. The paint is absorbed into the clay body and is there to stay. Usually the painter has his design in his head and knows just what he wants to paint. This varies, however, for some artists seem to make up their designs as they go along. A few of the younger artists draw their designs on paper first, and others sketch a rough outline on the floor before they work on the bowl or jar.

And now last of all comes the firing.

In a storehouse the Indians have piled away cakes of dry dung, or manure. It may be cow manure, horse manure, or sheep manure. The cakes of dung are very important in firing Indian pottery.

Out in an open space on the ground the potter builds a fire. This first fire is built to make sure that the ground will be dry before the firing of the pottery begins. The potter uses cedar wood for her fire and waits until it has all burned to ashes. Then she uses iron rods or an old stove-grate and places it on bricks or tin cans, so that the grate is raised a few inches above the ashes. The vessels which are to be fired are placed upside down on the grate. A wall of dung-cakes is built around the grate so that they do not touch the vessels. A roof of dung-cakes is built over the top, and now the oven is ready. More cedar wood is poked under the grate and the fire is started again. It is kept burning for about one half-hour, and then the cakes of dung are lifted off with pokers, and the vessels are lifted out with shovels or hay forks. They are placed on a tin to cool, and when they are cool enough to handle each piece is carefully wiped with a dry cloth, then with a greasy cloth or a chamois skin. The vessels are now ready to be stored away, carefully covered with a sheet to keep off dust and flies.

From the time that the firing begins till the vessels are removed from the oven and stored away, great care must be taken. They may be overfired or underfired and either would spoil the pottery. Finger marks and dust might leave unsightly spots. If the ground is damp or the fire does not burn properly, smoke may mark the surface of the vessels. Different potters have slightly different ways of firing their vessels and different wares require different handling. The polished black ware must stay in the oven longer than other wares, and before it is finished a tub full of loose manure is piled on top of the oven, filling all the cracks and keeping in the heat. This manner of firing causes the clay vessels to turn black.

Several different wares have been made by the Indians of San Ildefonso to sell to tourists and gift shops. There is, however, one ware that has become so popular that it is now crowding out all other wares in this village. This is the polished black ware with designs painted in dull black. Red clay is used for this ware and with ordinary firing it would remain red, but when it is finished with a smothered fire, oxygen is cut off and this turns the iron oxide in the clay from red to black. The paint used for this ware is Maria's invention, the yellow powder paint with a little guaco added to it. This yellowish or grayish paint also turns black in a smothered firing, but the paint turns a dull black which makes a beautiful contrast on the polished surface of the vessel.

Maria and Julian make beautiful pottery in this ware and their designs are usually quite simple. For this reason they are more pleasing to us than the elaborate designs of some other pueblos. Julian, especially, paints very simple patterns, sometimes only a row of scallops or dots around the rim of a bowl, but so carefully and beautifully executed that we are always satisfied.

The design elements used by the various potters of San Ildefonso have certain characteristics which are similar, but each potter makes her own designs. Some of the important elements, or motifs, are *avanyu,* the horned serpent; conventionalized birds or feathers; leaf patterns; scallops; triangles; frets; and terraced figures.

The favorite shapes of the San Ildefonso potters are the shallow bowl with incurved rim, and a deeper bowl with broad shoulders and a narrow mouth. They are learning, however, to cater to the white people by developing many shapes which are used for many purposes. We find jars designed to be used as lamp bases, and even cigarette boxes and ash trays.

The Hopi Indians of the First Mesa in Arizona are also

Acoma pottery, New Mexico.

Acoma pottery. 1900. Abstract and plant forms.

Zuni pottery. 1900. Deer in "house," with life symbols from mouth to heart.

Zuni pottery. 1900. Geometric border design. Main design, feather symbol.

Modern jar made at Sia, New Mexico. Notice similarity to Acoma pottery.

Pottery vessel — San Xavier, Papago Reservation, Arizona. Modern. Lugs, or handles, are probably in imitation of White Man's ceramics.

Pottery from Santo Domingo Pueblo, New Mexico.

producing large quantities of pottery for tourist sale. Their work is mainly a revival of ancient pottery, and, like the potters of San Ildefonso, they too understand the beauty of simplicity in design. By repeating a single motif in a continuous pattern around the top of a bowl or jar they obtain a beautiful effect. The scroll motif is very common, and also a crescent or horseshoe-shaped design. There are a large number of designs representing birds, both realistic and conventionalized.

Hopi ware is made of a clay which, when fired, has lovely shades of cream and yellow, often showing tones of soft rose. Hopi potters do not use a slip, but on this beautiful background paint their designs in brown and red. The workmanship on most Hopi pottery cannot compare with that of San Ildefonso, but their feeling for design is greatly admired, even by Julian, Juan, and Abel, who are the outstanding artists of San Ildefonso.

The village of Acoma in New Mexico is interested in making pottery for tourists, but, like their near neighbors, the Zuni, they are first of all interested in making water jars and a few other vessels for their own use. Acoma designs represent two distinct types, the naturalistic and the geometric. The first type is very simple and the design motifs are birds and plant forms. The color is red-on-white with all designs outlined in black. The geometric type is very elaborate and often confusing. The entire surface of the jar is covered with triangles, squares, diamonds, steps, and bands. These figures are sometimes filled in with narrow parallel lines which we call hatching. Quite frequently in Acoma ware the lower portion of the jar is plain red.

It has been difficult to interest the potters of Zuni in commercial wares, and consequently they are not especially interested in making any changes or improvements in their pottery. Large water jars are most often made, and the style is black-on-white with a small amount of red worked into some designs. Most noticeable in their decoration is the division between the neck and body of the vessel. A line, called the *onane,* or road, is drawn to show this division. The *onane* represents to the Zuni potter her span of life, and when drawing it on a pottery vessel the *onane* is not closed. If closed it would mean the end of her life. The favorite design motif found on Zuni pottery is the deer enclosed in a framework which is called his "house." Lines are drawn from the mouth to the heart of the deer to show that "the mouth speaks from the heart." Near the deer is sometimes painted a rosette design representing the sunflower. We also find birds and stylized butterflies and dragonflies. A feather-like design represents prayer-sticks. Geometric designs consist of steps, spirals, triangles, squares, diamonds, and circles with rings of scallops. Figures and spaces are occasionally filled with simple hatching or crosshatching.

The pueblos of Santa Clara and Santo Domingo are neighbors of San Ildefonso. Polished black ware is made in both of these villages, but in Santo Domingo the characteristic ware is black-on-cream. The potters use a beautiful clean slip and paint simple geometric figures in black. The cream spaces are large and the general effect is often very pleasing.

Other pueblos making pottery are Sia, Cochiti, Isleta, and Laguna. At Sia the dominant style is a decoration of birds and plants resembling the Acoma ware. Laguna is also influenced by Acoma. All of these pueblos, however, are mostly concerned with making cheap souvenirs for tourists.

POTTERY MADE BY THE INDIANS

Each pueblo has a dominant style with reference to form, color, and pattern of design, but most pueblos and most potters make more than one style. Although these styles are, in the main, extremely characteristic, there is today some borrowing of ideas and patterns. Over a period of years the styles are usually somewhat changed, and today there is a very definite trend toward meeting the outside market for their wares.

In the different wares the potters make bowls of many shapes; *ollas,* or water jars; prayer-meal bowls; double-mouthed vessels; double bowls; and vessels with handles. Some of these shapes they have made for many years. Frequently bowls and jars are shaped like gourds. Gourds are seed pods of certain plants. When dried, and the seeds removed, the pods make excellent drinking cups or vessels for holding or storing foods. Early Indians discovered this valuable plant and put its pods to many uses. It was quite natural that they should model pottery bowls and jars after the shapes of the gourd pods. The modeled shapes became traditional and are used today.

The prayer-meal bowls and a few pottery drums are made for ceremonial use, and the bowls have a very special shape and decoration. The rim is uneven and built up like steps, the decorations are symbolic and represent clouds, rain, lightning, and life forms which are in some way connected with water. The decoration on these vessels is usually very crude and no effort is made to get an artistic effect. The purpose of the design is simply to depict religious symbolism.

Among the Zuni, ceremonial bowls are of different sizes and are made with or without handles. The rim may have one, two, or four terraces. The large bowls are used for mak-

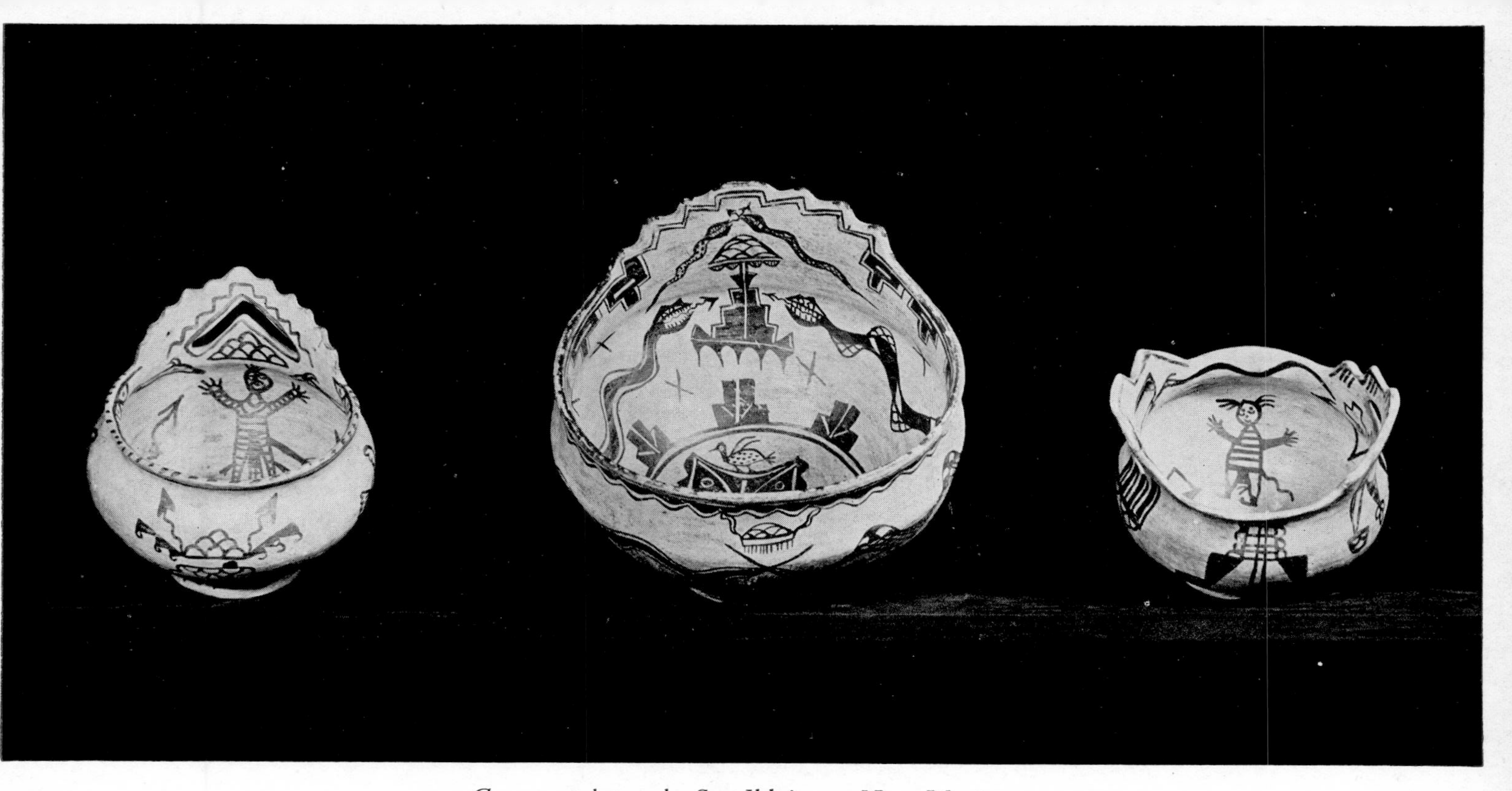

Ceremonial vessels. San Ildefonso, New Mexico.

ing yucca suds with which the Indians bathe before certain ceremonies. The small bowls usually hold the sacred white corn meal. All sizes are painted in black on a white slip.

Ceremonial bowls of a similar type are used by most of the Pueblo and Navajo tribes. The bowls have various uses because of the many and elaborate ceremonies which are performed by different tribes, but quite frequently they are filled with corn meal and other foods which are offered as a gift to the gods. Perhaps a new home is to be blessed and the corn meal is sprinkled around. Perhaps a Night Chant is to be sung by the medicine men, and bowls of corn meal have some part in the ceremony. For we must remember that to these people in the past, corn was the staple food, and that their corn crops depended on the rain. And so, rain-magic and the precious corn meal itself appear in nearly every ceremony. In *Waterless Mountain** by Laura Adams Armer, the author has told of two such ceremonies in a very beautiful way. In speaking of the blessing of a new home she tells how a young Navajo first silently offered the gift of corn to the house where he and his family would dwell. He then sprinkled the corn meal which he carried in a bowl, on different parts of the house, saying in a low tone:

May it be delightful, my house.
From my head to my feet
  May it be delightful.
Where I lie may it be delightful.
All above me may it be delightful,
All around me may it be delightful.
  May my fire be delightful.

* Used by special permission of Longmans, Green & Co., Publishers.

Accept this gift, Oh, Bearer of the Day.
May it be delightful as I walk about my house.

And then walking to the doorway he sprinkled the white corn meal toward the east, saying:

May this road of light ever and always lead
in peace to my home.

There was a time when the art of making fine pottery had almost died out among the Pueblo Indians. When the Spanish conquered the Indians of the Southwest, and later when the people of the United States moved westward, they carried iron kettles and tin pails with them. The Indians were very anxious to have these vessels for their own use, and as time went on they were able to obtain many things from the white people. The art of making beautiful things with their hands as their ancestors had done, was almost lost. And then a very fortunate thing happened.

About twenty-five years ago archaeologists became very much interested in the Southwest. They wanted to know what sort of people lived there in the past, and what sort of culture these people had. They knew that there were many ruins of old Indian villages, so they went out to study them. They found ruins "in all sorts of places, on the tops of mesas, in open plains, in narrow canyons, on the ledges of great cliffs, and in the shelter of caves." Some ruins showed that the village had been built of small houses of one room with walls of poorly made adobe brick. Others were great buildings of hundreds or even a thousand rooms, sometimes four

Zuni ceremonial bowl. New Mexico.

Banded-neck pitcher. Pre-pueblo. Mitten Rock, New Mexico.

Corrugated cooking vessel.
Aztec Ruin, New Mexico.

Pottery bowl. Pre-pueblo. Navajo Reservation, New Mexico.

or five stories high. The walls of these great buildings, or pueblos, were strong and well built. In New Mexico, Arizona, Utah, Colorado, and the northern part of Old Mexico, archaeologists have found thousands of places where prehistoric Indians lived and built their villages. Most of these villages were in ruins when the Spanish under Coronado made their first explorations in this part of the country. We do not know what happened to the people who lived in them, or how long ago the villages were occupied.

Before the time of the Pueblo Indians the Southwest was occupied by more primitive tribes, who are known as the Basket Makers. They had learned to weave baskets of yucca fiber, shredded roots, and wooden splints, which they sometimes coated with mud and ashes or with gum from the piñon tree. The baskets were of many shapes, and designs in red and black were woven in simple patterns. These very same patterns, whirls, zigzags, and straight line designs, appear on the oldest prehistoric pottery vessels found when excavations have been made. Because of this it is believed that the pueblo Indians conquered the Basket Makers, but adopted some of their ideas. The very earliest use of clay in making containers was to line the baskets which were used for storing foods. A thick layer of clay was pressed on the inside of the basket. It was a better protection against rats and other small animals or insects than the basket alone would have been.

The next step was to mix fibers of corn husks or bark with the clay, and model thick-walled vessels without the basket covering. Still later it was probably some accident that taught them the great value of firing their pottery. They learned to temper the clay, and to build up the walls of their vessels by means of coils. They could now produce pottery having thinner walls and more artistic shapes.

One of the earliest ideas of decoration was to leave the coils unsmoothed on the outside. This is known as corrugated ware and by some tribes was developed in highly specialized patterns. With the fingers geometric designs were pressed into the coils, and sometimes there would be as many as twelve coils to an inch. Bowls and jars have been found made in this way with such fine, even, and regular coil work that we marvel at the skill of the potter. This ware was not painted and was used largely for cooking vessels. Painted wares were not suitable for cooking because their colors were soon obscured by the smoke of the fire.

Time went on and the potters in the different villages developed their wares and created beautiful and interesting designs. Students of this old pottery can tell at a glance to which village it belonged.

Important archaeological expeditions have been carried on at Mesa Verde in Colorado; at Pueblo Bonito and the Aztec Ruin in New Mexico south of Mesa Verde; at Kayenta in north central Arizona; and at Tularosa and the Mimbres Valley in southeastern New Mexico. All of these pueblos were deserted before the Spaniards arrived and it is not known just when they were occupied.

The villages of present-day Indians are also very old, and in their neighborhoods are many old ruins once occupied by early members of their tribes. Near the present town of Zuni in New Mexico excavations have been made at the old ruin of Hawikuh. In the Rio Grande region of New Mexico near the village of the San Ildefonso Indians, excavations have been made in the Galisteo Valley and at Pecos. And on the first mesa in Arizona, where we find the Hopi Indians, excavations have been made at Awatobi and Sikyatki.

Pottery has been obtained from many other old pueblo sites, and owners of property have recovered some vessels and thousands of broken pieces when ploughing their fields or digging for building foundations.

There is a certain similarity in all prehistoric pottery of the Southwest, although outstanding characteristics were developed by each separate pueblo. The earliest decoration seems to have been suggested to the potter by the geometric decorations developed in basket-making. These designs were probably impressed in the corrugated wares by the fingers while the clay was moist. Simple geometric design appears on the earliest painted wares and very elaborate geometric designs on the later painted wares. It is most amazing to find lines, squares, triangles, spirals, frets, bands, dots, stepped and terraced figures, combined in every conceivable way to produce an enormous variety of patterns.

A favorite motif of design found on the pottery of many early pueblos is the bird. It was painted realistically in some designs, but more often was highly conventionalized and is quite difficult to recognize as a bird. The serpent and motifs representing feathers are frequently worked into early designs.

The very earliest prehistoric painted wares were probably all produced in the natural color of the clay from which they were made, and painted in black. Later a white or gray slip covered the vessels and black designs were painted on this white background. Thousands of pieces of black-on-white wares have been recovered from different ruins. In certain places have been found black-on-red, black-on-buff, and even

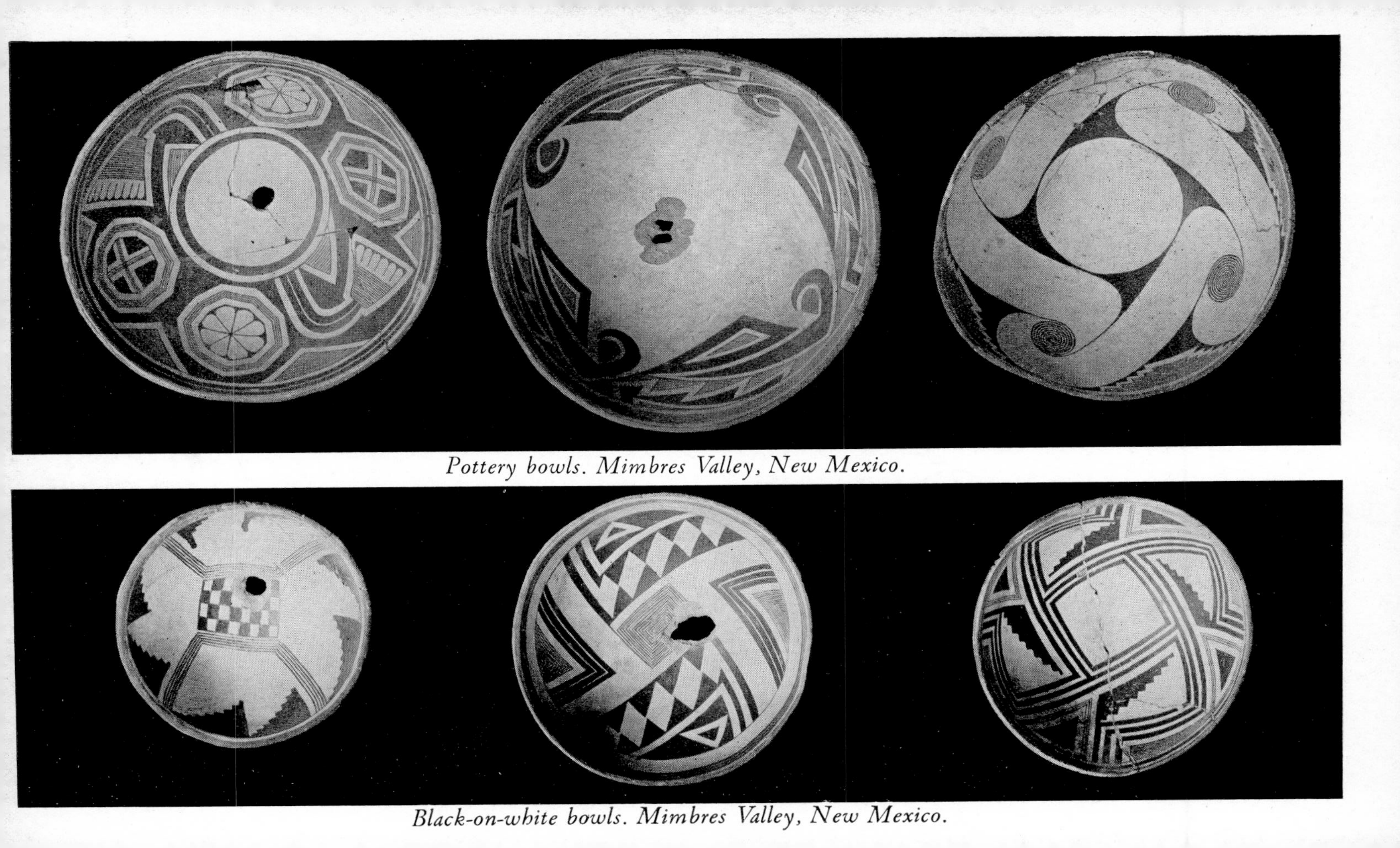

Pottery bowls. Mimbres Valley, New Mexico.

Black-on-white bowls. Mimbres Valley, New Mexico.

polychrome, or many-colored, wares. Some wares of three colors, perhaps orange, red, and black, or red, brown, and black, and still other combinations, are called polychrome. When excavations were made at Pecos the archaeologists were able to recognize twenty different wares of pottery.

On what is called red ware, the paste has been covered with a red slip, polished, and decorated with black. This ware, however, is not as common as the black-on-white ware.

In the valley of the Mimbres River have been found pottery vessels with black and white decorations which are most unusual and beautiful. Not only are the geometric designs elaborately and skillfully executed, but they often serve as a framework for beautifully painted realistic or conventionalized animal forms. Solid black and hatch work are combined in these designs, and we find depicted humans, fishes, birds, beasts, and insects.

Prehistoric pueblo pottery has been recovered which was decorated with a glaze-paint. This paint became vitrified in the firing, but was applied in lines and spaces for decoration only, and was never used to cover the vessels. It is thought by some that, if the Spaniards had not arrived, the art of the Pueblo potter would have advanced in time to the place where he would have discovered the value of a true glaze.

South of the United States in the state of Chihuahua is the ruin of Casas Grandes which is supposed to have been the southernmost town of the pueblo culture. And there has been found what is considered the very best of all prehistoric pueblo wares. Polished black ware, red ware with interesting incised designs, and vases in the form of gourds have been recovered, but the very finest pieces are painted in red and black on a smooth yellowish background. The designs are clean-cut and largely geometric in the form of spirals, scrolls, and frets.

Prehistoric pottery wares include vessels of many shapes and sizes. In our museums are bowls and jars, large and small, vessels with handles and without handles, vessels with one handle or several handles, pitchers, mugs and ladles, and sometimes pots with lids. The shapes are usually round or globular, but a few vessels have odd irregular shapes. It is thought that vessels having odd shapes were probably used for some religious or ceremonial purpose. At Pueblo Bonito 110 cylindrical jars were found in one room, and at no other ruin have jars of this type been found.

There is much discussion among students and archaeologists regarding the religious symbolism used on the prehistoric pottery, and on the pottery which is being made today. The Indian does not wish to talk to the white man about his religion and only a few people have gained his confidence in these matters. It is quite possible that in the past, birds, snakes, and other animals, mountains, rivers, clouds, and other forms of nature which he represented in his art, all had a definite religious symbolism. Today, however, it would seem that these design motifs have become merely traditional, and, except on ceremonial vessels, are used as best suits the fancy of the artist, for decorative purposes only. This is most certainly true regarding the pottery made for sale to the white purchaser.

To the early Indian of the Southwest all nature around him represented beauty. It was his life and his religion. Invisible spirits guided his actions and these spirits were pleased

Pottery bowls from Mimbres Valley, New Mexico.

Pottery from Tularosa, New Mexico.

when they were represented in the daily activities of the people. In this way symbolic designs came to be used.

The greatest need of the early Indian farmer of the Southwest was water. Prayers and ceremonies and artistic representations of the rain god were magic to bring the rain to their crops. Without this rain their crops would die. Without a good harvest the people would die.

We find, painted on their pottery, pictures of clouds, frogs, dragonflies, and other designs which expressed a wish for rain. The gods would see these pictures on the bowls and jars, and would know that the people needed help. The mountains could provide a safe dwelling place when an enemy came to steal the farmer's corn, and pictures of mountains acted as prayers to the mountain spirits. Certain animals, like the deer and the buffalo, would give their bodies to provide food for the Indian, if their spirits were pleased. Other animals had the power to give strength, skill, and endurance to the warrior. The sun and moon were the warriors' guides in time of war. Everything in nature had a spirit, and all these spirits must be continually flattered in order that they would help the Indian in his daily life.

Among all Indian tribes there seemed to be a feeling of the Earth Mother and the Sky Father in the realm of the many gods whom they worshiped. To the Indians of the Southwest this idea expressed itself in beauty, and the priests or singers of the tribe have made, for special ceremonial occasions, many beautiful poetic songs.

> Oh, our Mother, the Earth; oh, our Father, the Sky,
> Your children are we, and with tired backs
> We bring you the gifts that you love.

Then weave for us a garment of brightness;
May the warp be the white light of morning,
May the weft be the red light of evening,
May the fringes be the falling rain,
May the border be the standing rainbow.
Thus weave for us a garment of brightness
That we may walk fittingly where birds sing,
That we may walk fittingly where grass is green.
Oh, our Mother, the Earth; oh, our Father, the Sky!

Translated from the Tewa by Herbert J. Spinden
*Introduction to American Indian Art,** The Exposition of Indian Tribal Arts, Inc., New York City.

When excavations of prehistoric pueblos are made it is quite often possible to recover whole vessels or broken pieces which when put together make whole vessels. They are frequently found in graves. When placed beside the body they probably contained food for the dead, but some tribes had a very interesting custom of placing a bowl over the head of the body. A hole was knocked out of the bottom of the bowl in order that the spirit of the bowl could accompany the dead person to the next world and be of real service there.

In the neighborhood of prehistoric pueblos are usually found refuse heaps which contain thousands of broken pieces of pottery. These broken pieces are called potsherds and, when whole vessels cannot be obtained, potsherds are very valuable to the student in determining different periods of development.

In 1907 Dr. E. L. Hewett of the School of American Re-

* Used by special permission.

search began to make excavations at the ruins on the Pajarito Plateau. He hired Tewa Indians from San Ildefonso to do the digging. These Indians were very much interested in the potsherds which were found and seemed to understand many things about the designs. The Indian women were especially interested because they, as you know, were the potters. Scientists and artists who were interested, talked to these women and tried to get them to take ideas from the old pottery and make new pottery which would be like the old.

At first very little was done about it. The potters had been making water-pitchers, candlesticks, and rain gods which seemed to please the tourists, and it was difficult to find buyers for the more expensive wares which took more trouble and time to make. But a few potters were persuaded to try to revive the old art. Museums and artists bought the finest pieces, and finally some of the women became interested for the sake of the art itself. In 1920 the Museum at Sante Fe, New Mexico, worked out a plan to encourage the potters, and to make it pay when they spent more time on their work. The Museum bought the best pieces in each firing and paid more than the potters asked. The pieces were resold, at first without profit, in order that a fund might always be ready to buy from the next firing. Better highways approaching the pueblos, were later built and tourists visited this section of the country in greater numbers than ever before. The country at large became interested in the revival of Indian pottery, and with a ready market the potters learned that it paid to do less and better work and to charge higher prices. Maria Martinez became the very best potter in the village of San Ildefonso.

The work of Tonita Roybal, also of San Ildefonso, has

Black-on-white bowls from Aztec Ruin, New Mexico.

Black-on-white jars from Aztec Ruin, New Mexico.

Black-on-white water jar and pitchers from Aztec Ruin, New Mexico.

Black-on-white bird-form vessels from Aztec Ruin, New Mexico.

Black-on-white mugs from Aztec Ruin, New Mexico.

Polychrome pottery jars from the prehistoric ruins of Casas Grandes, Mexico.

recently come to the notice of those who are interested in Indian pottery. She uses Maria's invention of dull, or matte, decoration on polished black ware, and has made some beautiful modern interpretations of Indian design.

At Santo Domingo an Indian potter whose name is Monica Silva has become interested in reviving the old traditional patterns of her pueblo. Some of these designs she carries out in decorated black ware like that of San Ildefonso.

Before the time of Maria, Tonita, and Monica, Nampeo Polacca, a Hopi Indian woman, became rather famous for her skillful copies of old pottery excavated near her home.

Today in some of our best gift shops you can find beautiful pieces of Indian pottery. Many people are interested in developing this art among the Pueblo Indians. There are government schools where the girls are taught by Indian teachers, and the aim is to keep the pottery truly Indian in its style. The potters go to the museums and study the old prehistoric wares which are kept there, and, although they are urged to make their own designs, and sometimes to use new clays, their style is always Indian.

CHAPTER IV

POTTERY MADE BY THE PREHISTORIC PERUVIANS

WHEN the Spaniards came across the Atlantic Ocean to find gold in this new world they went not only to the southern part of our own country, but to Mexico, to Central America, and to South America. In these places they found natives who had developed wonderful cultures of their own. The Spaniards set about to conquer the natives and to take from them all riches which could be sent over to Spain.

The story of the natives as the Spaniards found them, of the Conquest, and what happened after the Conquest, was for many years almost a lost record. With the Spanish soldiers came priests who felt that it was their duty to destroy all signs of what they considered the heathen religion of these people. Every effort was made to convert the natives to Christianity. The soldiers and those who came later to govern the people and set up a new Spanish colony also felt that the sooner the people learned to live like Spanish people the better it would be.

Because of these attitudes on the part of the Spanish conquerors, the civilizations of the native Indians were practically wiped out. Their gold and silver were confiscated, melted, and recast in Spanish coin and ornament. Their precious stones were reset according to Spanish ideas of decoration.

Their fine hand-crafts ceased in an effort to comply with the demands of their conquerors, and because the people were discouraged and downtrodden. Their temples and works of art were destroyed because of the symbolic paintings and images, which would remind the people of the religion and beliefs of their ancestors. In times of war little thought is given to preserving valuable records, and willful destruction occurs wherever the conquerors subdue the people.

Today, however, archaeologists are coming to the rescue. Excavations are being made among old ruins, and ancient graves are being opened. Large numbers of pottery vessels, potsherds, and clay images have been recovered. Many of these are excellent records of the lives of the people.

In the year 1532 when Pizarro and his little band of Spanish warriors arrived in Peru there was a powerful empire which extended from northern Ecuador to middle Chile. The head of this empire was called the Inca. He was a great leader and was more interested in organizing and governing his people than in developing the arts. Pottery was made but it was not as fine as the prehistoric pottery which had been made before the Inca had conquered all the tribes around. People must have peace and some leisure time before they can develop really beautiful works of art.

So it was the people of Peru who lived before the time of the Incas who made the finest pottery. Sometimes by modeling figures, and sometimes by painting pictures on their pottery, they told many things about their ways of living. People who study these records can read them almost as surely as if they were in writing.

We believe that the Peruvians had not learned to write, but they used certain symbols, or marks, over and over again.

Human heads, animal heads, or just an eye, a foot, or a hand would have some symbolic meaning and represent, in many cases, some religious idea. It has been thought that these marks were hieroglyphs, but it is now generally accepted by students of these ancient cultures that the Peruvians did not have a real system of hieroglyphic writing.

There are four figures which the prehistoric Peruvians used more than any others in all their works of art — the bird, the fish, the puma, and the human figure. They are not drawn as they really look, but represent these animals and make most interesting motifs of design.

The Peruvians had many gods. The highland tribes and the coastal tribes, according to their needs, conceived different ideas of supreme deities. Indians living in the cool mountain districts felt the need of the warm rays of the sun to cause the growth of their crops, and they became sun-worshipers. The Incas called themselves the "Children of the Sun," and they believed that the founders of their race were the true son and daughter of the Sun. The coastal tribes were surrounded by deserts where the hot sun burned out the vegetation, and they believed that the moon was responsible for the night dews which made it possible for their crops to grow. They sat along the beaches on beautiful moonlight nights and watched the ebb and flow of the tide and expressed its mystery in the idea of a moon god. The sea also became a mysterious and sacred being to these early people, and was associated with the moon.

To most early people in different parts of the world animals were fearsome creatures and must in some way be persuaded to be friendly to man. This often brought about a deification and worship of animal gods. Most important to the early Peruvians were the puma god, the fish god, and the condor god. Paintings on pottery and designs woven in exquisite textiles represented these gods in elaborate and sometimes beautiful decorations. The puma god was represented as part man and part puma, the fish god as part man and part fish, and the condor god as part man and part bird. The condor is a large bird that lives in the Andes. There is a legend saying that Llira, whose husband abandoned her, prayed to Pachacamac, the creator-god, to help her. A fearful thunderstorm and earthquake occurred and Llira took this sign to mean that she had won favor with the god. She was about to sacrifice her son, Guayanay, to Pachacamac to show her gratitude, when a condor swooped down and carried the boy off to an island in the sea. There he grew up in beauty and later became the founder of the Incas.

As the civilizations of the early Peruvians advanced they worshiped creator-gods who were supposed to be all-powerful in sky, land, and sea. Pachacamac was the creator-god of the coastal tribes, and Viracocha the creator-god of the Inca and his followers.

It is told that a certain Inca looked upon the Sun from day to day, watched it rise in the morning and set in the evening, and conceived the idea that there was a greater power which controlled even the coming and going of the Sun itself. After turning this matter over in his mind the Inca consulted with his priests. They were filled with amazement but listened to their master and accepted the idea of a supreme creator-god. It was thought, however, that the great mass of the people would not understand this sort of god and for many years Viracocha was known only to the rulers and the priests.

AMERICAN INDIANS

POTTERY MADE BY THE PREHISTORIC PERUVIANS

Sir Clements R. Markham in his book on *The Incas of Peru** gives the following translation of an Inca hymn.

O Viracocha! Lord of the universe,
Whether thou art male,
Whether thou art female,
Lord of reproduction,
Whatsoever thou mayest be,
O Lord of divination,
Where art thou?
Thou mayest be above,
Thou mayest be below,
Or perhaps around
Thy splendid throne and sceptre.
Oh hear me!
From the sky above,
In which thou mayest be,
From the sea beneath,
In which thou mayest be,
Creator of the world
Maker of all men;
Lord of all Lords,
My eyes fail me
For longing to see thee;
For the sole desire to know thee.
Might I behold thee,
Might I know thee,
Might I consider thee,
Might I understand thee.

* E. P. Dutton & Co., Inc. Publishers.

O look down upon me,
For thou knowest me.
The sun — the moon —
The day — the night —
Spring — winter,
Are not ordained in vain
By thee, O Viracocha!
They all travel
To the assigned place;
They all arrive
At their destined ends,
Withersoever thou pleasest.
Thy royal sceptre
Thou holdest.
Oh hear me!
Oh choose me!
Let it not be
That I should tire,
That I should die.

We must keep in mind that in the coastal regions and up in the Andes Mountains were many groups of people, each group developing different ideas of the life about them. It is true that there were certain similarities in their cultures, but in many ways each group developed a different civilization. Travel was difficult and it was not until the time of the Incas that roads and bridges were built. Different tribes before the time of the Incas knew very little about each other.

Archaeologists have determined that the earliest civilizations in Peru grew along the coast. In southern Peru there was a civilization known as the Nazca culture and in northern Peru a civilization known as the Chimu culture. These two groups of Indians developed their cultures about the same time and it is now believed that they flourished between the years 100 B. C. and A. D. 600.

The very finest Peruvian pottery which has been recovered belongs to these early cultures. The potters of the Early Nazca period had a wider range of colors than has been found in any other part of South America. They used crimson, scarlet, pink, yellow, orange, green, various shades of blue, brown, gray, black, and white, and combined these colors in a truly artistic way. On many old pieces of pottery the colors are still bright and beautiful. The painting was carefully and accurately executed, and frequently represented the gods of the people. All these gods seem to be fierce and terrifying. Outstanding figure motifs have been listed as follows: the Spotted Cat, the Cat Demon, the Bird Demon, the Multiple-headed God, and the Centipede God. It is quite evident that the priests directed a religion which would frighten and awe the common people.

These god-creatures are frequently depicted with a protruding tongue. It is not known what this may signify. There is usually an elaborate headdress and a peculiar whisker-like mouth-mask. Hands and feet are represented with too few or too many fingers and toes. Ceremonial staffs, clubs, spears, spear-throwers, and slings are carried in the hands. Frequently two or three trophy-heads will be shown swinging from a spear or staff, for these people sometimes displayed the heads of their captives. The polychrome painting and the technique of design used by the potters and weavers of the Early Nazca period were not excelled by any group of American Indians, although their elaborate, fantastic ideas

Large ceremonial urn found in the Valley of Nazca, Peru. Tiahuanaco style. Design represents Viracocha, the creator-god. His "tears" are the rain, and the rays of the sun radiate from his face.

Figure of a condor. Muchik culture of northern Peru.

Pottery jar. $12\frac{3}{8}$ inches high. Nazca, Peru. Notice whisker-like mouth-mask.

Cup. Mythological character. Notice protruding tongue. Nazca, Peru.

of design are not always pleasing to us. There are, however, many vessels with simpler designs in which we see the human face, birds, fish, pumas, and other animals or insects highly conventionalized and arranged as geometric figures of design.

The pottery of this early period has thin walls and was skillfully fired. There is a great variety of lovely shapes and interesting designs. Especially noticeable are the many small bowls, cups, and shallow dishes which were evidently used for serving food and drink.

The Early Chimu potters have left a wonderful record of the daily lives of their people. Modeled forms predominate. These are sometimes painted, but frequently modeling and polishing is their only decoration. Jars, pitchers, water bottles, and various household vessels were modeled to represent practically everything that the people had or did. We know what fruits and vegetables they ate because we can recognize them in the modeled pottery forms. They have represented their houses, and the people themselves. They have shown individuals suffering from some accident or disease, others playing upon musical instruments, or caring for the animals which they had domesticated. The llama, which was their only beast of burden, was beautifully modeled in pottery forms.

Hundreds of little clay whistles have been found modeled in the form of a bird or an animal, and there are other musical instruments made of clay, such as trumpets.

The most amazing modeling was done in making portraits of the leaders of the people. Quiet, composed, beautiful heads were skillfully sculptured. Others show strength and power and still others arrogance and cruelty. One must see these heads to realize the exquisite workmanship of the artist potter.

Realistic painted pictures are found on modeled jars and on vases of simple shapes. These paintings represent ceremonial dances, battles, hunting and fishing scenes, cultivation of crops, travel in litters carried by slaves or workers, and the occupations of the women such as weaving and preparing of food. Costumes of priests, warriors, and workers are shown, as well as ornaments such as nose, mouth, and ear decorations.

The great mass of Early Chimu pottery is modeled or painted truly to represent some real object or occasion, but there are certain vessels whose decoration would come under the head of design. These may or may not be symbolic. The clay used was mostly reddish and was covered with a cream-colored slip. Decorations were painted in black, brown, or reddish brown. Faces, hands, and feet of human figures were frequently left uncovered with slip and showed the natural color of the clay.

Very characteristic of Chimu pottery water bottles is the stirrup handle-spout. Handles of this type became so generally used that they sometimes occur on what are thought to be objects not having a useful purpose.

The output of pottery vessels during the periods of the Chimu culture was so vast and so varied that many archaeologists have thought that it had some very special significance. Dr. Julio Tello, a noted archaeologist of Lima, Peru, has an interesting theory that the pottery vessels were used as records. Representing words or ideas the vessels could be combined or arranged in such a way that they would express any desired message or information.

POTTERY MADE BY THE PREHISTORIC PERUVIANS

Up in the highlands of Peru at the time of the Early Nazcas and Early Chimus a new culture was developing. In the neighborhood of Lake Titicaca the climate was suitable for the higher development of the native Indians. Necessary raw materials were at hand and the highland people were slowly rising to heights of civilization. There came a time when they extended their power over the coastal peoples and created an empire. This was the Tiahuanaco culture. Their pottery was usually painted in rich, dark colors often representing the puma god or the condor god. The puma was quite generally worshiped in all parts of Peru and it is thought to have been a symbol of the Sun.

Many portrait jars have been recovered which belong to this period. In the main they represent men with quiet, dignified expressions, whose features were similar to the higher types of Indians living in the highland district today.

About A. D. 900 there was a decline of the Tiahuanaco culture and the next period of importance began about A. D. 1100. Along the coast there arose what is spoken of as the Late Chimu and Late Nazca cultures, and in the highlands we find the beginning of the Inca culture.

The most distinctive pottery of the Late Chimu period is the polished black ware with designs in relief and figures in the round. There is also a polished red ware with similar designs. Here again we find the stirrup handle-spout. During this period the Chimu potters developed a double-bodied water jar which is very curious. It is modeled in two parts which are connected near the bottom so that the water can pass from one jar to the other. Usually on the top of the front jar is modeled a little animal and beside the animal is an opening which is formed in such a way that it becomes a

Portrait jar. Muchik culture of northern Peru. Interesting geometric design on cap.

Pottery jar showing modeled ears of corn. Lima, Peru.

Pottery vessel modeled to represent man of importance. Northern coastal culture. Peru.

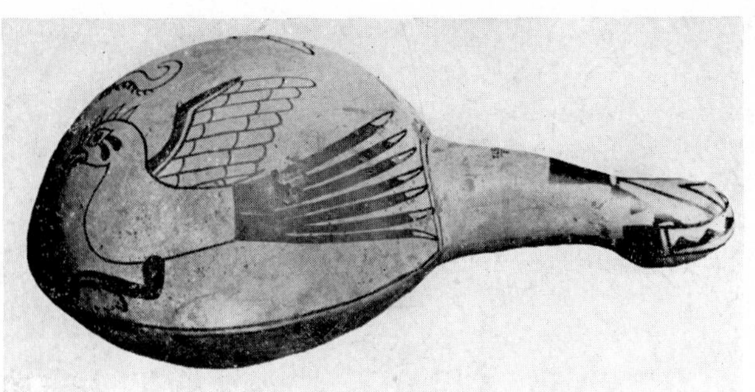

Corn popper. Norther coastal culture. Peru.

Pottery jar representing a human figure. Trujillo, Peru, a site of the northern coastal culture.

Mythical figures painted on a large, narrow-mouthed pitcher. Muchik culture of northern Peru.

Jar in shape of fish. Chimbote, Peru. Chimbote was a site of the northern coastal culture.

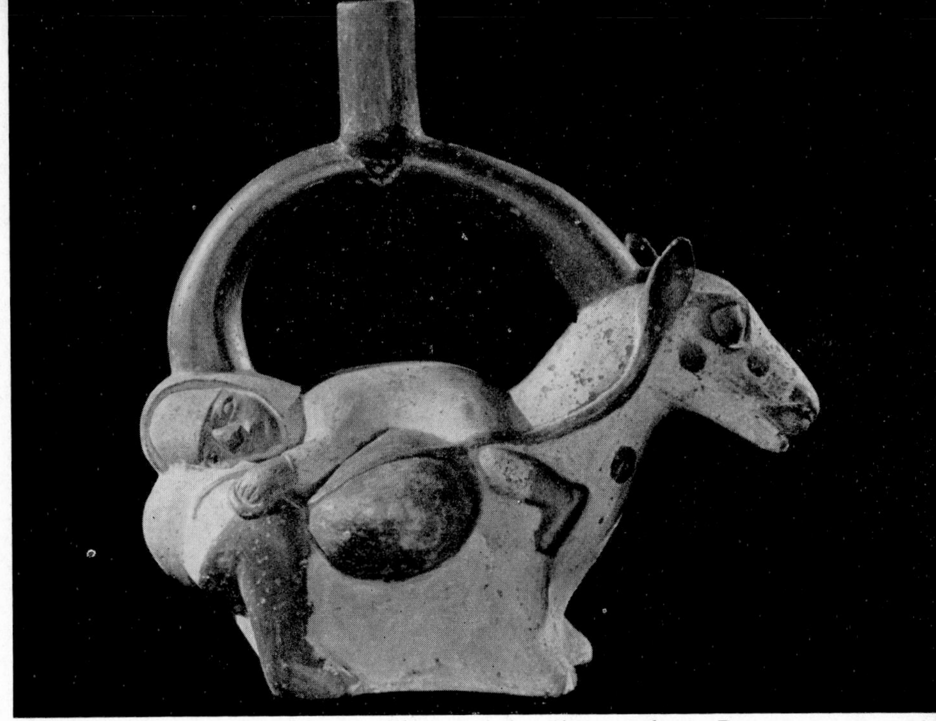

Pottery jar. Man on llama. Early Chimu culture. Peru.

Early Chimu portrait jar. Peru.

Pottery vessel in shape of human foot. Notice sandal. Northern coastal culture. Peru.

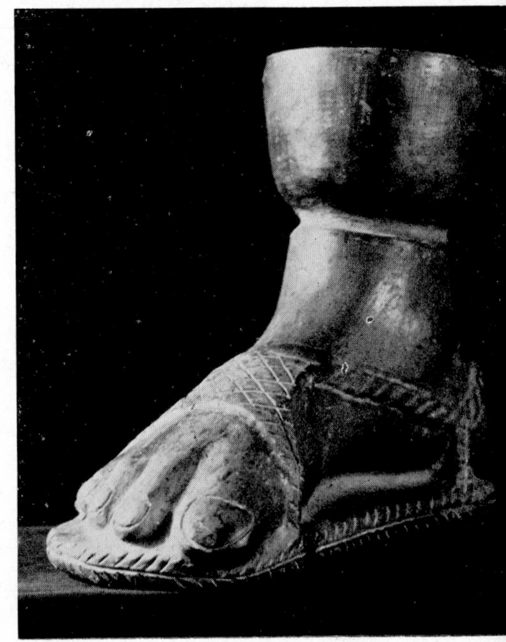

Figure of a Bird. Muchik culture of northern Peru.

Pottery vessel. Squash design. Northern coastal culture, Peru.

Double whistling jar. Probably Chimu culture.

whistle. Occasionally the jar itself is in the form of an animal. When the jars are partly filled with water and swung backward and forward, whistling sounds can be heard. Some jars will whistle when water is poured from one of the openings. The water forces the air through the whistle and makes the sound.

Whistling jars were also made by the Nazcans, and musical instruments from clay, such as flutes, trumpets, horns, Pan's-pipes, bells, whistles, and rattles.

Pottery design of the Late Nazca period is principally represented by geometric patterns inspired by the textile art. This new feeling for geometric designs is also found in highland art at this time and was the principal idea of decoration used by the potters of the Incas.

The Inca Empire dominated all of Peru from about 1400 to the time of the arrival of the Spaniards in 1532. These people had a wonderful genius for government and their history is a peculiar combination of consideration for, and oppression of, the people. All power was in the hands of the ruler, or Inca; every individual had what he needed according to his station in life, but any rebellion or disobedience was severely punished. Even members of the royal household had their share of work to do, and the Inca himself scorned a life that would make him unfit for battle and for the hardships of travel in going from one part of his country to another.

It is not difficult to understand that in an empire of this sort there were few luxuries for the common people, and for the ruler only those which were meant for personal adornment in order that he might appear gorgeously attired before his subjects.

Cast of pottery dish with modeled human figure in center of dish. Tiahuanaco style. Valley of Nazca, Peru.

Double whistling jars. Late Chimu black ware. Peru.

Pottery jar. Nasca, Peru. Well-spaced conventionalized design.

Pottery bowl with conventionalized spider design. 7 inches across top. Nasca, Peru.

Very large jar of aryballus *type. Peru.*

Pottery whistles. Colombia, South America.

The finest pottery of this period is a water jar known as the *aryballus,* so called because of its similarity to a certain Greek vessel. It has a graceful shape, and is painted with rich, dark colors in well-balanced geometric patterns. Usually a small knob at the base of the long neck is modeled to represent an animal head. This knob and the two handles near the bottom of the jar are used to hold the carrying rope when the *aryballus* is placed on the back of the worker. Sometimes only one side of the jar is decorated.

The Incas wore large ornaments in their ears. The important people had beautiful ornaments made of gold or silver, but the working people had ear ornaments made of clay. They were very heavy and the lobe of the ear was often stretched almost down to the shoulder by their weight. In early childhood the ears were pierced and tiny plugs inserted. As the child grew, larger plugs were used and the hole in the lobe of the ear enlarged. As an adult the lobe of the ear was simply a rim of flesh around a large hole. The usual shape of the ornament was a round disk attached to a spool-shaped plug which fitted into the hole in the lobe of the ear.

The Incans, like most of the Peruvian Indians, were very fond of music. Musical instruments were probably made from wood, cow's horns, and many other materials, but we know that certain instruments were made of clay. Some of these have been found, and are in our museums today. Modeled figures playing on musical instruments have also been found. An instrument like the pipes of Pan has always been a great favorite and today certain tribes of Bolivia make a huge form of pipes from three to ten feet long. Four or more Indians play together on this instrument.

POTTERY MADE BY THE PREHISTORIC PERUVIANS

To quote from *Old Civilizations of the New World* by A. Hyatt Verrill: "The present-day Indians of the Peruvian and Bolivian highlands are born musicians, and it is seldom that a man or a boy is without his beloved queña. As they walk along, bending under their burdens; as they drive their llama trains; as they hurry toward some fiesta or dance, they continually play the plaintive peculiar music of their Incan ancestors upon their Incan queñas or their Pan's-pipes. And wherever a boy or a man is tending the flocks of sheep, cattle, llamas, or alpacas, the centuries-old airs of the Incans will be heard, filling the rarefied mountain air with their melodies. Often, so bird-like are the notes, the stranger searches the stone-riddled fields and the barren hillsides for some unknown feathered songster, until he catches a glimpse of a brown-skinned mite wrapped in a tattered red poncho, and perched upon some outjutting rock overlooking the flocks and herds grazing upon the sparse dry herbage." *

Most of the Peruvian pottery which you will see in museums has been taken from the graves of the people, although thousands of broken potsherds have been picked up around old ruins. The coast region of Peru is a vast desert except where small rivers rising in the mountains flow through the desert on their way to the Pacific Ocean. In the valleys of the rivers lived the early Peruvians, but they buried their dead out in the desert. There is practically no rain in this region and the dry, nitrous, sandy soil is such that the dead body, wrapped in dozens of beautiful woven textiles, was naturally mummified and preserved. In these graves

* Used by special permission of the Bobbs-Merrill Company, Publishers.

were placed pottery vessels containing food, many of which were in perfect condition when excavations were made.

Representative pieces of pottery made during the different cultural periods can today be seen in museums in many large cities of America and Europe. We have not attempted to describe all the wares or all the types, but just those which are most characteristic.

In the Museum of Natural History in New York City is a fine collection of early Peruvian pottery. Of course not all the Peruvian pottery is beautiful. Some of it is crude and the forms seem to us quite ugly. But the very finest pieces have lovely shapes, beautiful colors, and well-made decorations. The largest pot in the Natural History Museum is four feet tall, and the smallest is only one-half inch in height. The tiny one was probably a child's toy.

The patterns of decoration on this pottery may seem queer to you. But if you look at the pieces which are considered fine, you will see that the designs are carefully made, and that the arrangement of lines and figures is very pleasing. The artist had a keen sense of balance. He knew where to place his lines and figures, and how to fill the spaces so that the finished work gives a feeling of satisfaction to those who are sensitive to the highest principles of art.

Although we cannot fail to appreciate the well-balanced shapes and designs, it is the color which truly astonishes us. Not only has the most exquisite taste been used in combining the rich reds, browns, and yellows, but, on many pieces, the colors are today as fresh as when they were painted. The artist potter generally used reds and browns on a cream-colored slip, but the polychrome pottery, especially of the

Early Nazca period, shows the use of a wide range of colors combined in an absolutely satisfying manner.

A number of pieces of modern Peruvian pottery were recently exhibited in a New York department store. The potters in some cases had tried to represent the designs used by the ancient Peruvians, but they had not succeeded in making the beautiful well-balanced designs which we find on the pottery made so long ago.

A friend who lives in Peru sent me several pieces of broken pottery which she had picked up where excavations were being made. The designs are very lovely. She said that there is no pottery being made today in Peru which can compare with the old wares.

Perhaps some day there will be a revival in Peru as there has been in our own Southwest. Perhaps some "Maria" or "Nampeo" may have real artistic ability, and perhaps someone will make it possible for these artists to sell their wares. We would then have in our shops lovely pieces of pottery with Peruvian designs. And these designs would be different from those made in all other parts of the world.

Blair Niles traveled through Peru, watched Dr. Tello carefully and reverently unfold the wrappings of a mummy, talked with the people, and examined their hand-crafts, both old and new. With much enthusiasm she wrote *Peruvian Pageant*, and from her book let us quote: "What has had true beauty endures beyond fashion and eventually lives again." *

* Used by special permission of the Publishers, The Bobbs-Merrill Company.

CHAPTER V

POTTERY MADE BY THE MAYANS

In the tropical countries of Central America there grows a tree called the chicozapote. From its sap we get a gummy substance which we use for making chewing gum. This gummy substance is called chicle, and so we have our practically new word — chiclet.

The peninsula of Yucatan is mostly covered with a tropical jungle in which grow many chicozapote trees. The native Indians who live in clearings in these jungles discovered that they could sell this chicle to the white people, and they made long journeys through the jungle to gather it.

The chicle gatherers came back from these trips with strange reports. They told of seeing ruins of wonderful buildings. Slowly the white people began to realize that the Mayan Indian who lived in Central America before the time of the Spanish Conquest must have had a very wonderful civilization.

Expeditions were planned and archaeologists began digging. At first it was thought that there had been just a few cities, but new sites are being discovered all the time. Many of these old ruins were found by the chicle gatherers. The Indians of Yucatan today are the descendants of the old Mayans, but they have forgotten all about the glory of their ancestors.

As old ruins were uncovered and old records brought to light, archaeologists came to believe that the Mayans had the highest form of civilization of all the Indian peoples. These ancient Indians erected marvelous buildings with beautiful carvings and painted pictures on the walls. Their priests studied the movements of the heavenly bodies and worked out a very accurate calendar. They had a system of hieroglyphic writing and kept a detailed record of seasons and dates. And they made beautiful things from gold, precious stones, and the brilliant feathers of the quetzal, a bird that lived in their forests.

As in other archaeological expeditions it was often the pottery which told stories to the diggers. In the land of the Mayans pottery and objects made of clay have been found in graves, in ruins of old buildings, and in caves. Excavations have been made in Coclé, Panama, where a prehistoric culture existed which was eventually covered by tufa and ashes from an erupting volcano. In this area an enormous number of potsherds have been found in remains that were evidently kitchen-middens, refuse piles, village sites, burials, ceremonial or temple sites, and mounds. The excavators found strata of potsherds from five to twenty feet thick.

It seems that the early people of Coclé buried their dead in a large pottery urn which they placed in a clay-lined grave. The body was cremated by building a fire in the grave. Into the fire the mourners threw beautiful pieces of pottery and stone tools which they valued. The "killed," or sacrificed,

Cylindrical jar painted in polychrome. Design shows quetzal and band of hieroglyphs. Height, $7\frac{1}{2}$ inches. Copan, Honduras.

Archaic clay figure, Mexico.

Figurines. Guanajuato, Mexico. From collection of Mrs. Ellen May Macomber.

pottery would probably frighten away the evil spirits. It is difficult for us to determine exactly what significance was attached to the ceremonial observances of these early people. It is evident, however, that they were extremely imaginative, that they greatly feared all natural forces, and were very superstitious. They lived in a land which was subject to earthquakes and volcanoes. And it is believed that this early culture was finally destroyed by a severe volcanic eruption.

Can you not picture the terror of the people when the earth rumbled and shook? Can you not see them rushing to the temple to sacrifice before the idols all their most cherished possessions? Many idols have been excavated and around them huge piles of potsherds and stone tools. Food was probably sacrificed at the same time, for among the broken pottery have been found many animal bones, fish bones, and sea shells.

It has been suggested that the survivors of the early people of Coclé might have been the ancestors of later Mayans of Yucatan. We will probably never know for sure.

Archaeologists believe that the Mayans and their ancestors had a civilization which lasted for almost 2000 years. During that period their ways of living changed many times. The pottery made by the early people was very different from the pottery which was made when the Mayan Empire was greatest.

The early pottery vessels had thick, heavy walls and very simple shapes. Quite often they stood on three little legs which were frequently hollow and contained pellets of clay making a rattle when the vessel was moved. Sometimes the legs were made to represent feet or faces, and sometimes the vessels themselves represented human or animal faces.

If you visit a museum exhibit of early Mayan pottery you will probably be most interested in the funny little human figurines made from clay. They are usually from two to five inches high. Many of them seem to represent Mother Earth and we think that the Mayans used them as offerings to the earth goddess, and to bring to her notice the need of the people for good crops. They were, perhaps, put into the ground when the seeds were planted. These little figurines are almost as flat as a gingerbread boy. Sometimes they are modeled to represent a figure with clothes on, and sometimes they are nude, especially the figurines of Mother Earth. Others have turbans, shirts, skirts, or aprons painted on the clay. Thousands of these little figurines have been found in the graves of early Indians who lived in Mexico, Central America, and northwestern South America. In his book on *Ancient Civilizations of Mexico and Central America,* Herbert J. Spinden gives a map showing just where these figurines have been found. You will also find many other interesting photographs and drawings in Dr. Spinden's book.

If you study these little figurines you will be surprised at the stories they can tell. They are crude and roughly made. They are surely not beautiful. But from them we learn what sort of clothes the people wore, what ornaments they had, and what they were interested in doing. Perhaps a man is modeled carrying a spear, or beating a drum. A woman is shown carrying a baby or a water jar.

Large figures of clay have been found in some graves. These are supposed to represent pictures of the dead.

Sometimes the figurines and other pottery made by these early people were painted in a very interesting way. The lines or designs used for decoration were put on with wax and then the object was painted all over. When the paint was dry the wax was peeled off. The design could then be seen in the natural color of the clay. This method of decoration is spoken of as negative painting and seems to have been used not only in Yucatan but from central Mexico to northern Peru.

Geometric design in simple lines and figures was used on early pottery. Realistic painting and modeling show animals and people in characteristic poses.

As the people became more highly civilized they made much finer pottery. Their ideas of religion took a more elaborate form and much of their art became symbolic, representing their gods, and relating to their religious ceremonies. Early forms of decoration were continued, but were more skillfully and artistically executed. We find painted and modeled shapes of gods, priests, and people; of animals, birds, and snakes. Designs were made with a carved wooden or clay stamp, and others with incised lines and figures. An interesting method of decoration was to incise the design deeply so that it had a carved effect. A few pieces have been recovered which are really carved in most elaborate design and show exquisite workmanship. On certain pieces the carving was done after the vessel was fired, and red paint was rubbed into the background. Flowers and heads were made in little molds and attached to bowls or jars in decorative patterns. The modeling of dishes with three little legs or feet was continued, but in more elaborate shapes and designs.

The objects we find most often represented in Mayan design are the serpent, which they worshiped; the quetzal, whose beautiful long feathers they used for decorating the headdress of a noble or a priest; their gods; and their hieroglyphs. The hieroglyphs not only told the story of the design, but were arranged in such a decorative way that they made a beautiful design in themselves.

Cylindrical vases with polychrome paintings of religious subjects are very beautiful. The background was usually painted orange or yellow, the designs outlined in black, and filled in with lovely shades of red, brown, and white. The surface had a very high polish, and great skill was shown in creating a truly artistic product. The method of firing produced beautiful shadings in the polished surfaces.

At first you may not enjoy the designs made by these ancient people. Their ideas were so different from ours. They represented their gods with strange figures which are part human and part animal. Their designs are so elaborate, with so many lines and curves, that you must look very closely to discover the ideas that the artist had when making his design. The serpent, quite often the rattlesnake, we think, was used again and again. To the body of the serpent would be added the long feathers of the quetzal, and human ornaments such as ear plugs or nose plugs would be placed on its head. Often you will find a human head in the open jaws of the serpent. In one section of the Mayan country the monkey was frequently used as a decorative motif, and in other places the jaguar and many different birds appear in painted, modeled, and carved ornamentation.

Dr. Spinden discusses Mayan art with reference to design, composition, and perspective. When our modern artists speak of design they refer to the pattern, or the arrangement of lines, spaces, and figures in a piece of work. To be good, a design must have some sort of order in arrangement of lines, spaces, and figures. Certain designs are created by very care-

Shallow bowl with cascabel *(rattle) legs. Polychrome painting. "Kill" hole in middle. Uaxactun.*

Drawing of design found Mayan vessel. Conventio owl and bat. Honduras.

ful measuring, and others by repeating one or more motifs in such a way that they make a rhythmic and continuous pattern. One part of a design must balance another part, and if color is used the tones and shades must be chosen in relation to each other.

When artists speak of the composition of a picture or a design they mean the selection and arrangement of what is to go into the picture or design.

The term perspective refers to the ability to draw or paint so that the object drawn or painted will have its natural shape and appearance. Little children are not concerned with perspective when they draw and paint. Neither are very primi-

Sculptured jar. Guatemala.

This beautifully carved vase is an example of the best period of Mayan art. The large head represents the Sun God. This head rests in the open jaws of a serpent which winds in and out around the vessel. The Death God is shown above. A second serpent, animal and human figures, and feathers cover the entire surface of the vase.

tive people. Look at the drawings of the early Egyptians and then at the carvings of the Mayas. You will see how much better the Mayas learned to represent the human figure as it really is.

Dr. Spinden calls our attention to the real beauty which

the Mayan artist achieved. He suggests that if we feel that the composition of their designs is overcrowded we should first try to understand what the artist wanted to represent. If we understand we will appreciate.

A very elaborate form of art is found on certain funeral urns which have been unearthed at Oaxaca, Mexico. It has not been determined just what the purpose of these urns might have been. When found they were empty but may have contained food for the dead. Usually several urns have been found standing side by side somewhere outside the burial chamber. Many of them are in perfect condition, but others seem to have had the hands purposely knocked off.

The urns are jars which are usually shaped like a cylinder. They vary in height from less than one foot to more than two feet. If you stand in front of the jar you cannot see it, for it is hidden behind an elaborate clay figure. Some of these figures represent human beings and some of them represent gods. Some were modeled to show how the person really looked and others have masks on. The heads are large and out of proportion to the body and there is a very elaborate headdress. Usually the figure is represented sitting with the hands on the knees or folded over the breast. All sorts of differences are shown in dress and ornament. Occasionally the urn is part of the body of the figure.

The Mayan religion required many and elaborate ceremonies, and many clay vessels were made and designed for some special religious purpose. Large jars for burning incense were used in the temples. These jars were often modeled in somewhat the same fashion as the funeral urns. They might represent the ceremonial masks or the feather headdress of the priests or the gods.

Pottery stamps. Mexico.

Incense burner. British Honduras.

In Costa Rica have been found incense burners in the form of large shallow clay pans with one long handle. The handle was generally modeled to represent an alligator or some other animal. These vessels were probably carried around during certain ceremonies, smoke rising from the burning incense and adding to the general impressiveness of the occasion.

Copal gum was used to furnish a white smoke, and rubber was used when the priests wished to produce a black smoke.

Not all things made of clay had a religious or a ceremonial significance. As we have said, figures were sometimes modeled to represent real people, and household utensils were decorated with geometric designs, painted pictures, and decorative hieroglyphs. Clay beads were made and sometimes

Pottery cover for jar. Costa Rica.

Clay Heads. Mayan culture. Salvador.

Funeral urn. Oaxaca, Mexico. Zapotec culture. Tiger god.

INCENSARIO. *Teotihuacan type. Valley of Mexico. Much restored.*

Laughing head. Figurine of clay. Vera Cruz, Mexico. Notice ear-plugs.

covered with real gold. Certain tools like spindle whorls, weights, and stamps for decorating cloth or the skin, were made of clay and many times beautifully designed.

We have come to recognize the culture of many different Indian tribes in southern Mexico and Central America. They frequently made war on each other and the conquerors would take over the cities of the conquered. They naturally influenced each other as they progressed to higher levels of civilization. Great similarities are found in their art and in their ideas of religion.

The Toltecs were a warlike people from the Mexican highlands, who at one time conquered the Mayans. They left a remarkable ruin at San Juan Teotihuacan in the Valley of Mexico, and there thousands of little clay heads have been found. Students believe that these little heads were used for religious purposes and that they were "attached to bodies made of some perishable material." There are many different kinds and it would seem that there are seldom two alike. Molds have been found, however, and occasionally two or three little heads made by the same mold.

At one time travelers could pick up any number of these little heads and carry them away. Today the ruins are protected by the government, but we can see and study the heads in museums both in Mexico and in our own country.

Other interesting pottery has been recovered from the ruins at Teotihuacan. There are dolls with head and body in one piece, and movable arms and legs; accurately modeled forms of the jaguar, the monkey, the owl, and other animals; and beautiful vases painted in soft greens, pinks, and yellows.

Cholula was a Toltecan city. Outstanding among its ceramic products were flat plates with beautiful polychrome designs. Other shapes were tripod vessels, cups in the form of an hourglass, and incense burners with broad mouths and loops near the base through which were passed ropes for suspending the vessel. Negative painting with applied wax was used, and on other wares engraved, or incised, designs were filled with paint of different colors.

In Guatemala and western Salvador prehistoric pottery has been found which has a so-called semi-glaze. Lead in the clay caused this effect when the pottery was fired. The Indians learned to use this particular clay for an interesting ware which they decorated with modeled forms and incised lines.

Although it is supposed that the finest pieces of modeled pottery found in Central America and in South America were made by hand, and that pottery vessels were usually built up by the coil method, a large number of pieces were made in molds.

The Totonacan Indians lived in the central part of Vera Cruz and excavations in their neighborhood have produced various types of pottery. Modeled clay heads with laughing faces are particularly interesting.

Other important cultures were the Tarascan, the Olmecan, the Mixtecan, the Zapotecan, the Chichimecan, the Chorotegan, and the Aztecan. Archaeologists are still working to determine dates and locations for these early cultures. It is now thought that the Mayans were the first to develop beyond a primitive stage. It is also thought that they went farther than any other group toward a high form of civilization. It is known that as early as A. D. 450 there were Mayan cities at Copán, Palenque, and Quiriguá, in the Highlands of

Geometric design taken from pottery vase. Salvador.

An interesting example of Salvador pottery which has the effect of being glazed.

A beautiful line design taken from pottery bowl. Salvador.

Polychrome vase. Mixtec culture. Oaxaca, Mexico. Design taken from hieroglyph for thirteenth day of the month.

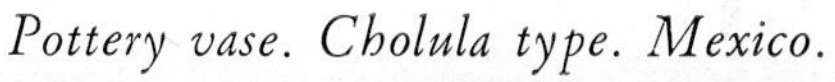

Pottery vase. Cholula type. Mexico.

Polychrome tripod jar. Tuscaran. Honduras.

Pottery bowl from State of Michoacan, Mexico. Certain vessels had little decorati-
but notice how carefully and accurately the shape has been modeled.

Polished red ware. Michoacan, Mexico.

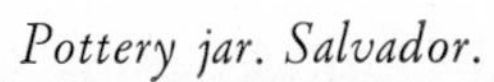

Pottery jar. Salvador.

Guatemala and Honduras. It is also known that for some reason these cities were abandoned and new cities were built in northern Yucatan about A. D. 1000. Here in Chichen Itzá, Uxmal, and other cities the Mayan culture flourished until about 1200 when they were conquered by the Toltecs.

The Toltecs in turn were overcome by the Aztecs who, in A. D. 1370, founded a city where Mexico City now stands, and which the Aztecs called Tenochtitlan.

When the Spanish arrived the glory of the Mayans was on the decline. Like most of the middle American tribes they were, at that time, in subjection to the Aztec Emperor Moctezuma. During the 2000 years of the Mayan supremacy the cultures of the near-by tribes were influenced by the Mayan culture and many similarities are found in their arts. When the Aztecs rose to power they in turn influenced surrounding cultures.

CHAPTER VI

POTTERY MADE IN MEXICO IN THE PAST AND IN THE PRESENT

Mexico City is situated on a high plateau and has one of the most delightful climates in the world. Interesting stories are told of the early tribes of Indians who strove to gain possession of this very desirable location. At one time it was thought that the Aztecs of Mexico and the Incas of Peru were the only Indian tribes which had developed real civilizations on this side of the world. It is now known that in the countries of Mexico, Central America, and northwestern South America there were hundreds of cities occupied by settled, more or less civilized tribes. At times they warred with each other and their civilizations rose and fell.

Those who were in power in Mexico City when Cortez came from Spain were called Aztecs. During the Conquest, when Spain conquered Mexico, the leaders of the Aztecs lost their power, many of them died in battle, and others were captured by the conquerors. Some of the Aztec women later married Spaniards and a new race of people grew up. But there were thousands and thousands of Indians who stayed Indians and lived very much as they always had done. Even today this is true. There are many Indians in Mexico

Mexican potter modeling a jar. The jar rests on a little stand which he turns with his feet as he works.

Clay figure. Mexican. Woman selling fruit in market place.

today who live just as the poor people lived in the days when the Aztecs were a mighty nation. For of course there were many poor people then too.

For a long time before the Spaniards came the Indian people had made pottery bowls and jars and dishes for their own use. Everything they had was made by hand. They wove beautiful cloth and decorated it with lovely embroidery. They carved wood, and made wonderful ornaments from gold, silver, and precious stones. And they made pottery of many different types and for different uses.

The Mexican Indians of today are still making beautiful things by hand. Today, however, they do not have gold and silver and fine materials. They use what they have, are always interested in color, and have a real understanding and appreciation of design.

Mexico is a tropical country and not all parts of it are pleasant places to live. But up in the highlands are many places which have a climate similar to that of Mexico City. The early people found these lovely spots and there they built their towns and cities. At first each town or village made everything which the people of that village needed, for of course in the beginning they were very primitive people. But as time went on they learned to trade with other people. Then those who lived where good clay could be found made quantities of pottery, took it to their markets, and traded for other things which they needed. After a long time the custom grew up that in one family they made only jars, and in another family only cooking pots, and so on. Then the people in the town traded with each other. And in some places this is just the way it is today.

In the small towns and villages the potters work in their

homes just as they have for long centuries of time. The clay is kneaded with the feet and the molding is nearly always done by hand. In pre-Spanish days the finest pottery had a very high polish, but many vessels for cooking and household purposes were made of common terra cotta.

The Spanish taught the natives how to make and use a glaze which gave their pottery a glossy finish, and prevented water or other liquids from seeping through the vessels after they were fired. All earthenware is porous and must have a glaze in order to make it entirely watertight. For the *olla,* or water jar, this porous quality is an advantage. The evaporation of the water through the body of the jar keeps the water in the jar cool. But for vessels which are used for preparing or serving foods porousness is a decided disadvantage. Particles of food are absorbed into the body of porous vessels and they soon become unsanitary.

The glaze used by the Mexican Indians today is made of tin, lead, and fine sand. Much of their pottery is glazed on one side only, and some of it has no glaze at all.

The village Indians make quantities of simple clay dishes for their own use, and bring their surplus into the larger towns and cities on market days to be sold at the great open fairs which are the delight of the natives. Many holidays, or fiestas, are observed by the Mexican people, and the open-air market is an important part of such occasions. The country people walk for great distances to attend a fiesta. Little burros walk patiently beside them loaded with dishes, or baskets, or toys. Hours have been spent in making these things, but they will probably be sold for a few cents. Time means little to the Mexican Indian and he gets real pleasure from his craft-work.

POTTERY MADE IN MEXICO

Mexico, after the Spanish Conquest, was for many years a very backward country. The great mass of her population lived very simply, and in the towns and villages there were almost no modern improvements. On the streets water carriers went about with large clay bottles strapped to their backs. These bottles, or jars, were made with several small loops of clay on the shoulder through which the strap was passed. In Guanajuata today the water carrier and his bottle can still be seen. He carries a little cup and a ladle. The customer samples the water and if he finds it fresh and cool he buys the contents of the bottle.

Until quite recently the church was the dominating factor in the lives of the Mexican Indians. Old customs in relation to the church are still carried on to a great extent. Candles are carried to church in pottery candlesticks and placed on the altar by worshipers. Decorated pottery bowls or jars are filled with incense, and the sweet scent of the burning incense fills the church.

Candlesticks and *incensarios* are also placed in the cemeteries on special occasions. Many of these pieces are black with a shiny glaze, and decorated with flowers or birds in relief. On November 2nd the Indians have a festival which they call the Day of the Dead. At this time food is placed in the cemeteries for their dead, and special dishes must be used to hold the food.

At Christmas-time new jars are bought and filled with nuts and candies. They are then covered with a papier-mâché figure and are ready for the fun. A person who is blindfolded breaks the jar and they all scramble for the candies and nuts. These jars of candies with their papier-mâché covers are called *piñatas* (pee-nya-tas).

Another Christmas custom which is carried on by the people of Oaxaca is to fry a very thin pancake in lard until it is crisp. The pancake is served in syrup and after it is eaten the plate is broken. "The more the pieces, the better the luck for the coming year."

All dishes, candlesticks, and *incensarios* used for special festivals must be new. You can see that this makes extra business for the potters. It is quite probable that this breaking of dishes and obtaining a new set was in the first place a matter of sanitation. Before the use of a glaze on their household vessels, common earthenware dishes would, as we have said, absorb particles of food, and soon become unfit for use.

Thousands of little clay figures are made to represent Christ in the manger, and the people and animals gathered around the manger. Some of these, for the poor people, are very crude and inexpensive, but the more expensive ones are beautifully made and very artistic.

The Mexicans have learned that they can sell many of these little clay figures to tourists, and they now make them to represent all sorts of workers in their country. Perhaps you have seen some of these little figures. Often they are very charming. We find them made not only of clay but sometimes of wax, and these are especially lovely.

The Indians delight in making their children happy. In the village markets and the city stores are "thousands of wonderful toys that even the poorest Mexican children may have." Many of these are made of clay. There are clay animals with whistles in their tails, and clay animals with slots in their backs so that the children can save their centavitos — when they can get them. Most of the Indian children are so poor that they use the little bank just as a toy.

POTTERY MADE IN MEXICO

Recently thousands of these little toy banks in the shape of fat pigs, gaily painted, have been sold in our gift shops. Interest in this little toy was probably stimulated by the publication of Mrs. Morrow's charming little book *The Painted Pig*. Quite frequently in our department stores there will be a special display and sale of Mexican arts and crafts. There may even be a young Mexican girl ready to explain the various articles on display. Among woven articles, lacquered trays, and ornaments of tin you will be sure to find pottery from one or more localities. Each ware will have its characteristic decorations. Most of it will be fragile and certainly not highly developed as to technique. But, almost without exception, if the ware be truly Indian, the colors will be pleasing and the feeling for design satisfying.

Besides the crude but artistic clay products made in the homes of the native Indians, there are in many places in Mexico pottery factories which supply the people of the cities with dishes, vases, and tiles.

In these potteries, or pottery factories, the Indians are the workers. They work very much as they do in their homes, but in the potteries they have brick ovens for firing, a few extra tools, and better ways of managing their work so that they can make quantities of vessels or tiles.

The factories were started by the Spaniards not long after the time of the Conquest. An interesting story is told of the founding of the city of Puebla which is an important ceramic center. In 1529 the first Spanish bishop of the Catholic Church came to this heathen land, says an old account, and assisted in a project to found a new town somewhere between the coast and the City of Mexico. Making this trip was a long and tiresome jaunt through tropical lowlands, and a resting place was needed. The bishop was considering just where the new town should be built, when one night he had a dream. In his dream he saw a beautiful plain crossed by two rivers, and as he gazed, two angels with line and rod measured distances and laid out plans for buildings, streets, and parks. Then the bishop awoke. He walked and walked until he found the spot he had seen in his dream. And there the city of La Puebla de los Angeles (the City of the Angels) was built.

Another old record says that a priest of early Puebla was anxious to erect a church which would be as beautiful as the churches in Spain. He had noticed that the native Indians were skilled workers in clay and he believed they could be taught to make pottery and tiles as the Spanish made them. He sent a request to his brother priests in Talavera, Spain, and asked that instructors come over and teach the Indian workmen to make clay tiles like those made in Talavera. Several priests who understood the work of the potter came to Puebla and in a short time that city was the center of a flourishing ceramic industry.

The earliest products of these factories were probably tiles, made after the fashion of Spanish tiles in the City of Talavera, and because of this the Mexican pottery was often called Talavera ware. Spanish Talavera ware was inspired by the tin enameled pottery which was made at that time in Italy, and the Italian ware was called maiolica. Today some people speak of all wares, whether antique or modern, which have burned tin in the glaze, as maiolica. And so the name Mexican maiolica is most frequently used.

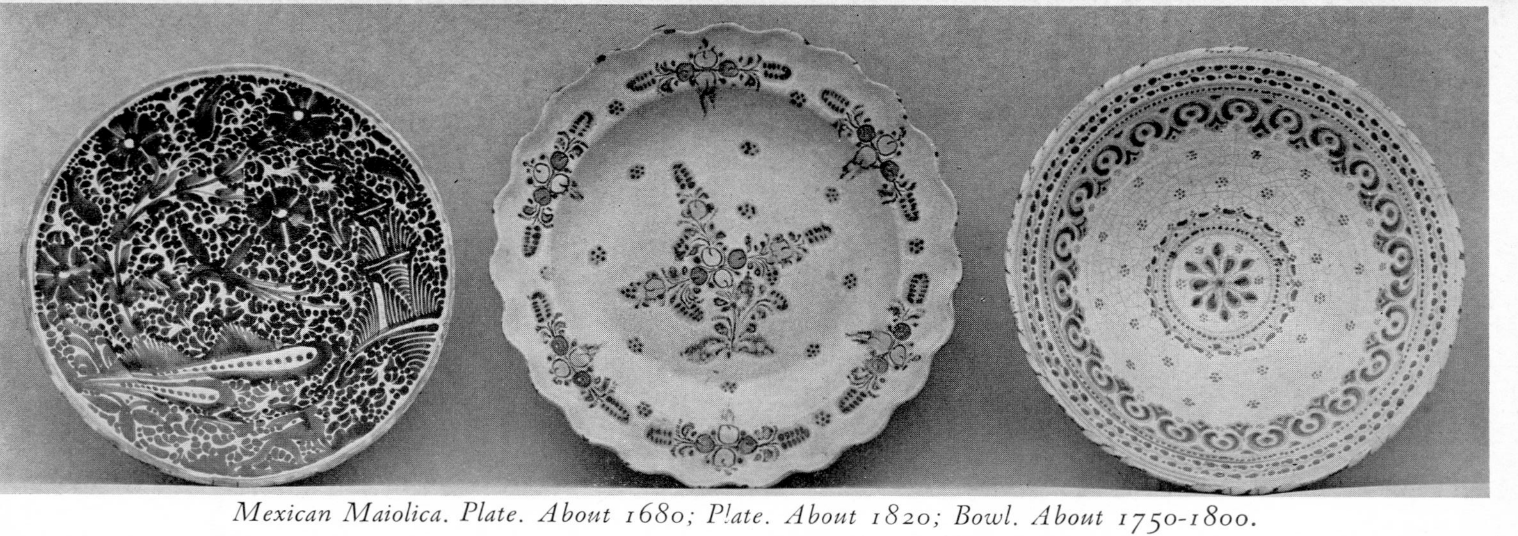

Mexican Maiolica. Plate. About 1680; Plate. About 1820; Bowl. About 1750-1800.

Sand-shaker. About 1750; Saltcellar. About 1840; Inkstand. About 1700. Mexican Maiolica.

Mexican Maiolica. Tile lavatory. Polychrome decoration with vases of flowers and escutcheon of Franciscan Monks. About 1830. From church of San Francisco, Puebla, Mexico.

Burned tin in an enamel glaze makes a white opaque covering and completely hides the natural color of the clay body. On this white enamel covering can be painted decorations in one or many contrasting colors. The early Mexican maiolica was painted in a deep, rich, dark blue, sometimes outlined in black, and the designs were like those used in Spain. Conventional floral and bird designs occur most frequently. We see the fern leaf on many old pieces, and sometimes animal and human figure motifs.

Since it was the priests who directed this work in the beginning, it is to be expected that the oldest and finest products were made for the churches, convents, and other buildings under the supervision of the Church. Many old churches with tiled domes are standing today in Mexican cities. Anita Brenner in her Mexican guidebook* says, "From a distance Puebla is quite worthy of its angelic surname. Plenty of people have been thrilled to verse at the sight of its blaze of maiolica domes, massed like a great nestful of Easter eggs in dark green moss."

Tiles were used not only for the domes of churches but for decorative entrances, garden walls, and patio floors. Interiors were also decorated with tile, especially altars, lavatories, and prayer nooks. Elaborately decorated maiolica basins fitted into the lavatories and were used by the priests when administering the mass.

Not only tiles were made in these early factories but vessels and vases of many shapes for use in the church buildings, and later for use in private homes. Our museum collections include bathtubs, or cisterns; *benitiers,* or holy water basins;

* *Your Mexican Holiday*, quoted by permission of G. P. Putnam's Sons, Publishers.

Mexican Maiolica basin. Design shows Moresque influence. Inscription on rim: "Soy para labar los puryfycadores y no mas." *("I am for the washing of the purificators and for no other purpose.") Date, 1650.*

Above, *Mexican Maiolica. Covered bowl. About 1820.*

Left, *Mexican Maiolica. Albarelli, or drug jar. Raised blue decoration. 18th Century.*

Below, Left. *Mexican Maiolica. Urn-shaped jardinière and a large bowl. About 1830.*

Below, Right. *Mexican Maiolica. Benitier*

covered dishes; inkstands; sand-sprinklers; saltcellars; candlesticks; flower vases in the shape of Italian *albarelli,* or drug pots; jardinieres and flowerpots used in the gardens, or patios; and large storage jars for storing liquids, vanilla, chocolate, and other foods.

As you observe these vessels in the museum let your imagination wander back to the days of their usefulness and you can picture many an interesting custom of the past. A bathtub was, of course, a luxury; *benitiers* were attached to the wall at the entrance of Catholic churches; sand was sprinkled on a written page to blot the ink; and burning candles were essential in the rituals of the Church. The Mexican people have always surrounded themselves with flowers, and some of their most precious foods were and are those which the Aztecs before them had cultivated and used. Storage jars have been found with hinged iron lids having a lock and key, and this was definitely because of the Chinese influence at that time.

During the seventeenth and eighteenth centuries all the potters of Europe became interested in the beautiful ceramic wares made by the Chinese people. They were so very interested that they copied the Chinese designs on their own pottery. This happened in Mexico too.

Although dark blue on a white background has always been extensively used for Mexican maiolica, many old pieces are decorated in dark blue, green, and yellow. Then came a period in which blue, green, yellow, red, brown, purple, and black were used, and still later other colors. These polychrome wares were apt to be gaudy and overdecorated. The European influence was still strong, and if we study the rococo decoration favored in Europe during the eighteenth century we will understand the current fashion of that time in Mexico.

By the middle of the nineteenth century, maiolica products became so highly commercialized that unskilled workmanship was often employed and a period of decadence set in.

The modern city of Puebla is still the center of the maiolica industry, and dishes, tiles, and tile panels are made. Although we can see influences of the old wares, Puebla maiolica has today characteristics which are truly Mexican and as such are different from pottery wares made in all other places.

It would seem that we have gotten far away from our Indian potter. But he was a very important factor in these early potteries and still is in the maiolica factories of today. He was the worker and many times became more skilled than his teachers. Remember his family had probably been potters for many generations before the Conquest. The success of the early maiolica depended on the skill of the Indian potters. The use of a true glaze and of the potter's wheel were introduced by the Spanish potters and the native Indian worker soon made them part of his own potting.

The chief centers of the pottery industry in Mexico today are found in or near the cities of Guadalajara, Tonala, Guanajuato, Cuernavaca, Puebla, Oaxaca, and Mexico. In these various districts are made many types of ceramic products, with many styles of decoration.

Guadalajara is the capital and largest city of the state of Jalisco and with its neighboring towns is probably the most important center for the popular types of Indian pottery. In this state Tonala is best known as a pottery town but San Pedro Tlaquepaque is also important. From Tlaquepa-

Mexican Maiolica. Panel of tiles. 17th–18th Centuries.

Mexican Maiolica. Chinese influence. 19th Century.

Mexican Maiolica. Blue & white. Chinese influence. 1680-1700.

Hunters and animals among foliage. 20th Century.

que come many interesting painted clay figures, animals, and fruits. The fruits may be arranged in a bowl for table decoration, or strung up in decorative groups for wall ornaments. They lend a lovely touch of bright color to a room or an outdoor patio. At other times they, like the clay animals, may have a slot on the top or side and may be used by the children to save small coins.

Guadalajara and its neighbor Tonala produce dishes, ornaments, toys, and miniatures. Here we find several styles of hand-painted decoration and glazing. There are three families which supply the artists for the best work. The Galvan family are makers of a blue-gray, blue, and buff, unglazed ware; the Lucano family are makers of a yellow glazed ware with palm, deer, rabbit, and fern designs; and the Panduro family are makers of miniatures, portraits, and caricatures. Portraits and caricatures of Henry Ford, Uncle Sam, George Washington, Pancho Villa, Carranza, or your own portrait if you choose to pose for it, are the delight of certain members of the Pandura family.

One finds in Mexican markets the most attractive and artistic miniature pottery. Dishes, vases, bottles, and figures. Tiny little animals, beautifully modeled. The Mexicans of all classes love these little ornaments, and a home of the poorest or the finest may have a shelf of such bits of ceramic wares.

One visitor to Mexico brought back the most exquisite little toy animals. She watched the toy-maker at work in his village home and she learned about his method for modeling his tiny objects. First he goes out in the field and gets the clay that he needs. He models the body, neck, and head of a horse, dog, cow, or some other animal. From this form he makes a two-piece clay mold. When the mold dries it is

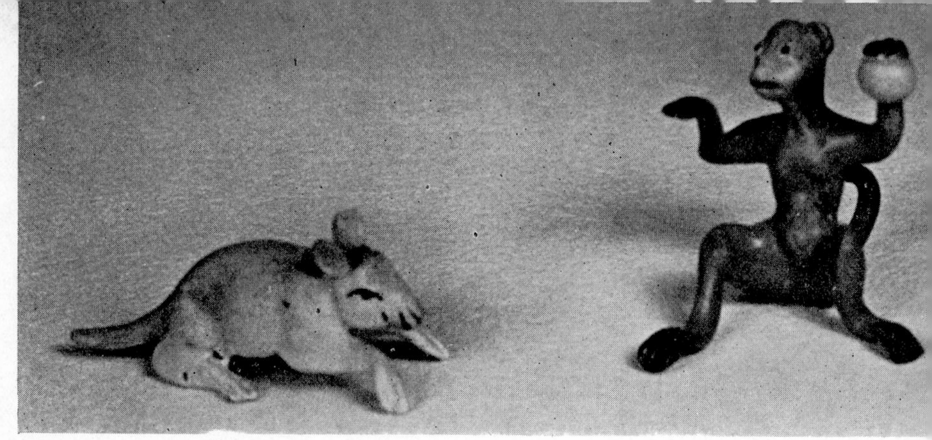

Miniatures made by modern Mexican potter.

baked and is then ready to use in making a number of duplicates. Thin strips of clay are pressed into the mold, covering all parts carefully. When partially dry the two pieces are removed and fastened together. The toy-maker now has the hollow body, neck, and head of a little animal. Tiny pieces of clay are shaped in his fingers for ears, legs, and tail, perhaps the head is turned slightly to one side, and the result is a very lifelike little creature. They are baked in a small charcoal stove, and when removed from the oven are allowed to cool and are then ready to be painted. Along comes a man who is on his way to the market and the potter sells these little figures to him for fifteen cents a dozen. They are beautifully and skillfully made and it is a pity that they are so fragile and so easily broken. But the potter's joy is in the making. He can always make others, and no matter how many he makes there will be some little difference in each figure. A change in the turn of the head, the swish of the tail, the position of the legs, or in the painted decoration.

From Tonala come quantities of common pottery of the type used by the poor people. This ware is the natural color of the clay with a high glaze and decorated with touches of cream, green, black, brown, or blue. Simple lines, birds, animals, flowers, names, sentimental thoughts, or even verses are found painted on pottery of this sort. It is made not only at Tonala, but in many towns and villages in other parts of Mexico. In our gift shops you will find it spoken of as ovenware. A variety of this ware is entirely covered with a cream ground and designed in color. Every conceivable shape and size used and needed by the Indian is made in this common pottery and displayed in outdoor markets. We must not forget that in the home of the Mexican Indian, clay vessels are used not only for the purpose of serving and storing foods, but for practically all kinds of cooking; thus we find clay pots and pans, and bowls and jars of many sizes and shapes. Some with covers and some without. Boiling, frying, roasting, and baking are accomplished in pottery vessels, and quite frequently the stove is made of clay tiles.

An important product of the Quadalajara district is the water bottle, many times with a small cup inverted over the neck, serving both as a drinking vessel and as a protection for the contents of the bottle. Beautiful vessels of this type are made by the Galvan family in soft grays and reddish browns and decorated in whites and blues.

Pottery from Guanajuato is a hard-fired ware and is usually dark brown or green in color. Figures in relief are frequently used for ornamentation. Certain potters make tiny toy dishes in this ware.

Miniatures made by modern Mexican potter.

POTTERY MADE IN MEXICO

Not far from the city of Cuernavaca is a small village where practically every family is a potter's family. The name of this little town is San Antonio, and Elizabeth Morrow in her beautiful book *Casa Mañana** speaks of "the potteries of San Antonio where the wheel runs all day long under flowering trees." The potters of San Antonio make quantities of cooking pots and water jars, little earthenware stoves called *braseros* in which charcoal is burned, and earthen gridirons called *parrilas* on which tortillas, or corn cakes, are baked. But these potters also make ornamented jars and vases, characteristic motifs of design being the lizard and the eagle.

Not far from San Antonio is a prehistoric carving of a lizard nine feet long on a huge boulder. A little farther away is another stone carved like an eagle with wings outstretched and ready to fly. These old carvings have inspired the Indian artists and they have reproduced them on their pottery in a very interesting way. With tiny pieces of broken pottery, sometimes with pieces of imported china, they have made inlaid designs showing the lizard and the eagle. Another favorite decoration in this ware is the Mexican coat of arms — the spread eagle resting on a cactus bush and holding a serpent in its mouth.

Puebla is the center of maiolica wares, and dishes, tiles, tile-panels, and ornamental pieces are made. There are copies of the old wares, and sometimes very poor variations of the old styles which might be called modern. Some are skillfully executed, others are carelessly produced. The prices are low and the factory owners are not always concerned with truly artistic products.

Tile work is probably just as popular today in Mexico as

* Quoted by special permission of the Author.

it was in the colonial days when Spanish gentlemen first built their homes in the beautiful valleys in the highlands. Where people have such a delightful climate they are quite apt to live outdoors the greater part of the time. Again I must quote Mrs. Morrow who said, in speaking of Cuernavaca, "The shabbiest door opens into a sunlit patio gay with tiled fountain and flowers," and then mentioned "a proud blue and white tiled fountain with old Aztec rabbits dancing in the center."

Not only tiled fountains are found in Mexican patios, but tile pavements, tile pools, and sometimes tile walls. Balustrades are made of unglazed terra cotta and large jars stand around to hold flowers and growing plants. And all are made by Indian potters.

Puebla also produces a black ware which is highly glazed and has raised ornamentation and fluted edges. The shapes are, many times, pre-Spanish and are imitations of gourd forms.

Southeast of Puebla is the city of Oaxaca which is also an important pottery center. An outstanding ware of Oaxaca is dark green with a high glaze. Toys and ornaments are made in this ware, as well as dishes. Recently in this green ware a design has been created which was inspired by the old Indian designs found on near-by ruins. Not far from Oaxaca are the ruins of Mitla which was the burial place of the Zapotecan kings. Tombs in the form of a cross have been unearthed and these tombs are lined with cut stones arranged in very interesting geometric patterns. Similar geometric patterns are today painted in cream color on a light brown pottery.

The town of Coatepec near Oaxaca City makes black pot-

Modern pottery jar. Mexican. Cream on light brown. Height, 18 inches. Design taken from stone mosaics in tombs unearthed at Mitla.

"Ovenware." Red clay, partially glazed, decorated with black and white.

Plate. "Ovenware." The common pottery of the Mexican Indian. Red clay decorated with cream color and touches of green.

Water bottle and cup. Polished earthenware with polychrome painting. Geometric design in old Aztec style.

Plate of dark gray earthenware. Modern reproduction of old Aztec des done in relief.

tery which is without glaze or decoration. Beautifully formed water jars and animals with whistles in their tails are outstanding in this ware.

The states of Mexico and of Michoacan contain many pottery towns and villages. Metepec in Mexico State is noted for a black glazed pottery painted in bright flowers. Many toys are made in this ware.

Pottery from the state of Guerrero is decorated in black lines and figures on a cream ground and is unglazed. Large jars and incensers are shaped and decorated many times in pre-Spanish style. Birds, flowers, and simple geometric patterns are used, with much of the cream background uncovered by design. Many jars stand on three little looped feet. Toys and other types of pottery are produced in this state.

In several states of Mexico we find that the principal city

odern plate with deep blue glaze. Design painted in polychrome, outlined in black. A recent development from the Guadalajara district.

has the same name as the state. This is at times confusing. Pottery is usually characteristic of a certain district or state although similar wares may be made in several districts and many types in any one district. In our country where manufactured products are used almost exclusively, and certainly wherever inexpensive pottery must suffice, it is difficult for us to realize what large quantities of these simple handmade pottery vessels, ornaments, and toys are produced in the various Mexican districts.

There are artists and archaeologists in Mexico today who recognize the contributions made to present-day civilization by the ancient Aztecs, Mayans, Zapotecs, and other Indian tribes. They are teaching the people to be proud of their heri-

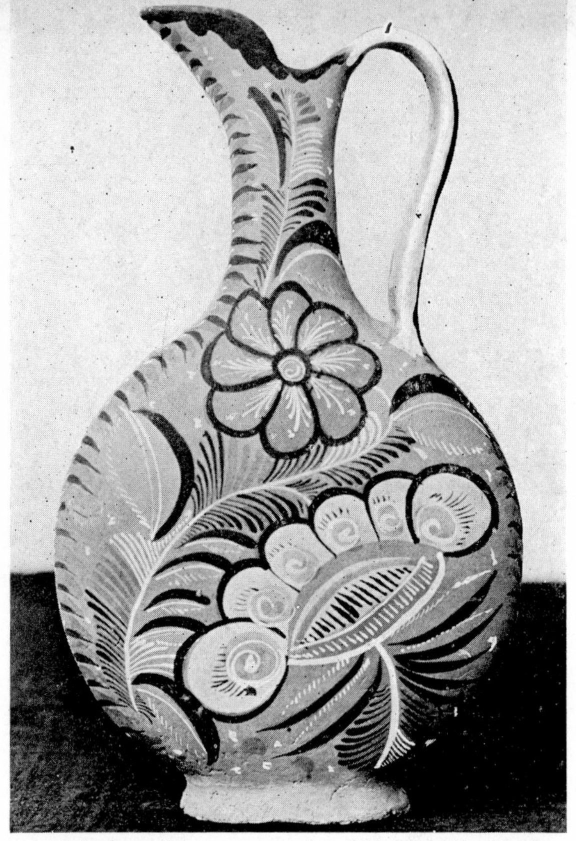

Modern Mexican pitcher. Unglazed. Crude earthenware painted in lovely shades of blue, tan, green, and white.

tage and to revive the old arts and crafts. They are also interested in archaeological expeditions which are excavating old ruins and making it possible better to understand and appreciate the early civilizations.

Pottery obtained from these old ruins is placed in museums for all to see. Potters and artists study not only the bowls, jars, and figurines which they see in the museum cases, but also the historical records which have been worked out by the archaeologists. They read about the lives of their ancestors, the foods which they ate, the clothes which they wore, and perhaps the most significant of all, the religious ceremonies which they observed. The Aztecs believed in many gods and these we find represented in modeled figures, and painted on their pottery, as well as carved in stone to ornament their temples. The serpent was worshiped here as among the Mayas. The jaguar, the eagle, the sun, and the moon. In fact they had a god to represent everything which they considered beautiful or powerful. There was a popular belief in the Earth Mother and the Sky Father and all of these gods were at times confused with priests and men. Human sacrifice was offered to the gods upon many occasions. Elaborate ceremonies and the burning of incense impressed the common people with the importance of their religion. These special occasions called for many types of ceremonial vessels which were usually made of carefully modeled or painted pottery. Earthenware whistles, rattles, and other musical instruments were used at these celebrations.

In the daily lives of the people there were many demands for pottery with careful, artistic design, and for pottery simply made with little or no decoration. The finest pottery during the Aztec period was made of red or orange clay and was finished with a high polish. Tripod, or three-legged, shapes were common. There were two distinct types of design; conventionalized designs of gods and religious traditions painted in polychrome, and geometric designs painted in black.

The more highly developed types of pottery made in pre-Conquest days are no longer produced, but new examples of these early wares are continually being added to museum collections as the result of archaeological finds. It is hoped by some folks that the Mexican potters will get renewed inspiration from these old Aztec vessels, and that in Mexico there will be a revival similar to that in the pueblo district of the United States.

There is, however, a diversity of opinion on the part of different individuals concerning this Aztec and Mayan revival. With news of archaeological finds there is much curiosity aroused and commercial potters take advantage of this popular interest to produce wares which will meet the fancy of fashion. Such pottery is made in large quantities, is the result of mere imitation, and is usually unskilled in its production.

A third group of interested people feel that the Indians are no longer a part of the early life and therefore cannot honestly express in their art a true feeling for the old designs. They would encourage the Indians in their simple forms of hand-craft and help to create a market which will bring to the potter better prices for his work.

It has been said that nine out of ten Mexican Indians are natural artists working at some sort of hand-craft. They express what they see and feel, simply and sincerely. Their skill has made it possible for them to adapt and apply the art of many nations, but if left to their own devices, the results will be most truly their own. They have a natural skill, an understanding of the principles of design, and a feeling for beautiful color combinations. They love deep, rich color, but gaudy colors are never truly Indian. The needed materials are near at hand, and there is an ever present market among their own people.

Mexico is today throwing her doors wide open to tourists. New roads are being built, and traveling is correspondingly simpler than in the past. Accommodations are better and Mexico has much to offer in the way of scenery, climate, and

Lower part of label for Calendar Stone. Drawing by H. J. Spinden. The god with the protruding tongue is found in different Indian cultures. It has been suggested that when used by the Aztecs this symbol represents the bloodthirsty Sun God lapping up the blood of his victims.

"The Painted Pig." A slit in his back makes this fat little pig a bank for small coins, or a receptacle for discarded razor blades.

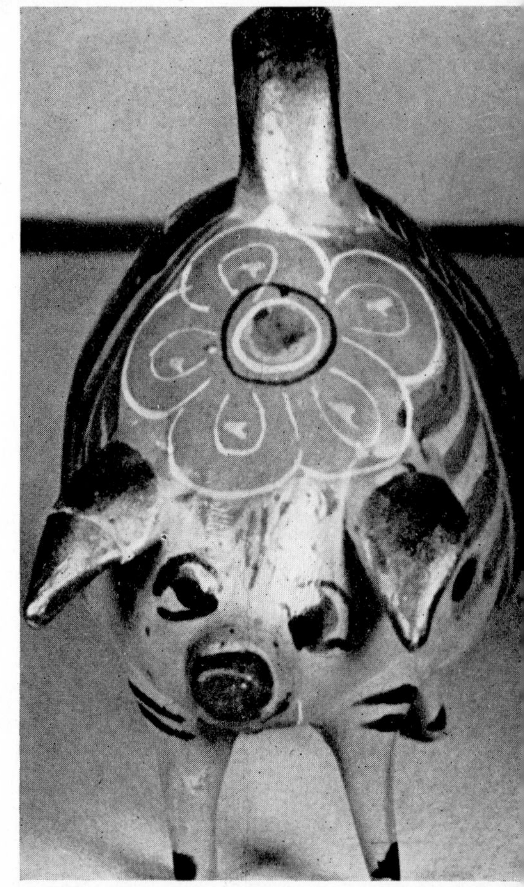

Wouldn't his expression delight the heart of any child!

Vase representing the God Macuilxochitl, Five Flower, the Mexican god of games and feasting. Oaxaca, Mexico.

Black-brown bottle. Pre-Spanish. Gualupita, Cuernavaca, Mexico.

Pottery rattle, 12 inches long. Oaxaca, Mexico.

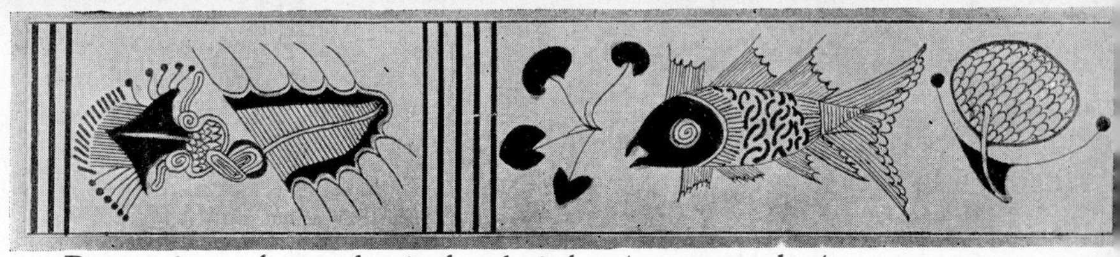

Design from the inside of a bowl of the Aztec period. A marine worm, water plants, and a fish are shown with clear recognition of their species.

points of historical interest. This means, of course, that many inferior products will be placed on the market to catch the eye of the tourist. Too often this class of traveler is responsible for the breaking down of artistic hand-craft products.

Mexico is making an effort to educate her Indian people, not only in book learning but in better ways of living. With a desire for greater comforts and more healthful living the Indian must provide himself with a larger income. Will he then be able to afford to spend hours fashioning a pot, a jar, a bowl, or some other much loved piece of hand-craft?

We have illustrated crude pottery and highly developed pottery of prehistoric natives of America. We have discussed the lost arts of some tribes, and the revival in our own Southwest. We have shown the importance of pottery vessels to the Mexican Indian of today, and the widespread interest in his simple clay products.

Not all Indian pottery is worthy, and not all Indian design is beautiful. It has an historical interest for the student, and, at its best it has an aesthetic value for the artist. For hundreds of years, in certain tribes, making and decorating clay objects was one of the most important means of artistic expression. It is remarkable that after a period of 400 years since the land of the Indian was taken over by the white people, there are today Indian potters who are still capable of producing a distinctive type of art. This art is recognized as a definite contribution to our present civilization, and is today receiving encouragement from many sources.

BIBLIOGRAPHY

FOR FURTHER READING AND EXTRA ILLUSTRATIVE MATERIAL

If you wish to do more extensive reading on this fascinating subject of Indian pottery, your city library will probably furnish you with extra material, although you may be obliged to hunt articles in magazines, or chapters in books on the general subject of American Indians.

Extra illustrative material may be your principal interest, especially if you do not live in the neighborhood of an Indian museum. Books that are written for collectors or for scientific students many times have illustrations which are of interest to all of us. The art department of your library is quite likely to have large-size books with large-size plates representing in color the many interesting types of clay vessels and figures which have been developed by the American Indians. Excellent photographs are sold by many museums for prices ranging from 15 cents to 50 cents. The 50-cent size is usually quite large, perhaps 8 x 10 inches, and suitable for framing. Colored prints are more expensive and not available in all types of pottery.

Dorothy Smith Sides has done a beautiful collection of paintings showing decorative pottery motifs. These paintings have been placed in a portfolio by the Fine Arts Press, Santa Ana, California. The title is *Decorative Art of the Southwestern Indians,* and the date is 1936.

The magazine *Design* for Nov., 1937, and for Dec., 1937, has articles and excellent photographs and drawings of Indian pottery and pottery designs.

Kenneth M. Chapman of the Laboratory of Anthropology, Santa Fe, New Mexico, has made an intensive study of the pottery of the Southwest. His book, *Pottery of Santo Domingo Pueblo,* contains over 1000 designs from Santo Domingo pottery. This book was published in 1938 and sells for $4.00.

Alida Sims Malkus has written a beautiful story about a Zuni girl, her family, and her lover. The Indian mother is an expert potter and much of the interest in the story is centered about the difficulty in obtaining an unusual pink clay for the mother's potting. This book is well known, is published by Harcourt Brace and Company, Inc., and is entitled *The Dragon Fly of Zuni.*

In 1931 a beautiful book was prepared for and copyrighted by The Exposition of Indian Tribal Arts, Inc., New York City. The book is entitled *Introduction to American Indian Art* and includes the following articles: —

Introduction to American Indian Art
by John Sloan and Oliver La Farge

Fine Arts and the First Americans
by Herbert J. Spinden

Indian Symbolism
by Herbert J. Spinden

Indian Poetry
by Mary Austin

Modern Indian Painting
by Alice Corbin Henderson

Sand-Painting of the Navaho Indians
by Laura Adams Armer

Indian Pottery
by Kenneth M. Chapman
Indian Sculpture and Carving
by Neil M. Judd
Indian Masks
by Chas. C. Willoughby
Indian Basketry
by E. W. Gifford
Indian Weaving
by Mary Lois Kissell
Indian Porcupine-Quill and Beadwork
by Wm. C. Orchard
Books on Indian Arts North of Mexico
Compiled by Ruth Gaines

Your interest may lead you to a study of some phase of Indian life other than the work of the potter. If you are interested in the Mayan Indians do not fail to see the beautiful illustrations in color in the *National Geographic Magazine* for November, 1935, and for November, 1936. Excellent illustrations of the Aztecs are shown in the same magazine for June, 1937, and the October, 1936, number gives a beautiful picture of the quetzal resplendent in its brilliant green feathers. Its tail plumes formed the elaborate headdress of the Maya chiefs, and today the bird is the symbol of Guatemalan freedom. It is used in the designs on the Guatemalan coat of arms, on coins, and on stamps.

The National Geographic Magazine for November, 1937, has a splendid article on "America's First Settlers, the Indians," by Matthew W. Stirling who is chief of the Bureau of American Ethnology, Smithsonian Institution, Washington, D. C. Accompanying this article are illustrations representing the Indians of the Northeastern Woodlands as they lived during the colonial times and the days of early occupation by the white man.

The American Museum of Natural History, New York City, publishes excellent material which not only gives information about Indian pottery, but about all outstanding phases of Indian life. The following guide leaflets and handbooks you will find most helpful:—

The Indian of Manhattan Island and Vicinity. By Alanson Skinner. 63 pages, 27 illustrations. Price, 20 cents.

Indians of the Southwest. By Pliny Earle Goddard, Ph. D. 201 pages, maps, and many illustrations. Cloth, 75 cents.

Pottery of the Southwestern Indians. By Pliny Earle Goddard, Ph. D. 30 pages, 22 illustrations. Price, 15 cents.

Peruvian Art as Shown on Textiles and Pottery. By Charles W. Meade. 24 pages, 9 full-page plates. Price, 10 cents. Contains interesting drawings showing conventional development of realistic motifs of design — fish, bird, puma, human figure.

Old Civilizations of Inca Land. By Chas. W. Meade. 141 pages, many illustrations and a map. Cloth, $1.00.

Old Peruvian Art. By Heinrich V. Doering. A beautiful book with full-page illustrations, several in color. This book is for sale at the Natural History Museum, but is published by E. Weyhe, 794 Lexington Ave., New York City. 1936.

Ancient Civilizations of Mexico and Central America. By Herbert J. Spinden, Ph. D. 270 pages, 75 illustrations. Cloth, $1.00.

Arts and Crafts in Central America. By George C. Vaillant. 102 pages, many excellent illustrations. Price, 35 cents. This leaflet is especially helpful to those who are interested in the arts of the Mayans and their neighbors. A valuable bibliography is appended.

Susan Smith has written an interesting little book called *Made in Mexico.* It is concerned with the folk-arts of the Mexicans, and remarks about pottery appear on almost every page. It is published by Alfred A. Knopf, New York, 1930.

INDEX